DEADLY PERILS

First published in Great Britain in 2009 by Bloomsbury Publishing Plc.
Published in the United States of America in 2009 by Walker Publishing Company, Inc.
Visit Walker & Company's Web site at www.walkeryoungreaders.com

For information about permission to reproduce selections from this book, write to
Permissions, Walker & Company, 175 Fifth Avenue, New York, New York 10010

Library of Congress Cataloging-in-Publication Data
Turner, Tracey.
Deadly perils : and how to avoid them / by Tracey Turner ; illustrated by Ben Hasler.
p.   cm.
ISBN-13: 978-0-8027-8738-5 • ISBN-10: 0-8027-8738-X
1. Safety education—Juvenile literature. 2. Accidents—Prevention—Juvenile literature. I. Title.
HQ770.7.T87 2009   613.6'9083—dc22   2009005605

Printed in China by Printplus Ltd.
2 4 6 8 10 9 7 5 3 1

FSC
Mixed Sources
Product group from well-managed
forests and other controlled sources

Cert no. SGS-COC-003853
www.fsc.org
© 1996 Forest Stewardship Council

DEADLY PERILS

AND HOW TO AVOID THEM

TRACEY TURNER

illustrated by
BEN HASLER

Walker & Company
New York

CONTENTS

Small but Lethal

Black Widow Spider
Killer Bees
Anopheles Mosquito
Death Stalker Scorpion
Giant Centipede
Tsetse Fly
Army Ants

Everyday Perils

Getting Dressed
Electricity
Poisonous Garden Plant
Sleepwalking
Botulism

Perilous Weather

Lightning Strike
Tornado
Blizzard
Sandstorm
Flash Flood
Freak Wave
Giant Hail
Hurricane

Adventurous Perils

The Bends
Altitude Sickness
Skydiving
Shipwreck
Cave-in

Don't Panic!

INTRODUCTION

In this book you'll find yourself in a series of alarming predicaments, all of which end very badly indeed.

Perhaps you've already considered deadly perils such as lightning strikes, crocodile attacks, and earthquakes. But you should also explore the dire consequences of some less obvious (but no less deadly) perils. Like being . . .

. . . struck by frozen toilet waste
. . . speared by a warty ghoul
. . . disemboweled by a large flightless bird
. . . overcome by a freak wave

Or how about the hidden hazards of getting dressed, eating, and going to sleep?

In addition to the grim details of what might become of you in a selection of terrible catastrophes, you'll also find advice on what you could do to avoid disaster. Discover how to deter an aggressive cassowary bird, outswim a rip current, survive a raging sandstorm, and recognize the telltale signs of an impending avalanche.

So pack your emergency supplies and put on your protective headgear: you're about to be bludgeoned, bitten, harpooned, poisoned, and incinerated . . . among other things. The next time someone asks you "What's the worst that can happen?" you'll be able to give them an informed reply.

MENACES FROM THE DEEP

Even Olympic swimmers are no match for the astonishing variety of deadly sea creatures that glide swiftly and efficiently through the world's rivers, lakes, and seas. Even more unfortunately for you, some of them are capable of poisoning you or biting you in half without even moving . . .

Peril: Box Jellyfish

Peril rating: 8/10

Location: Northern Australia, West Indo-Pacific, Southeast Asia

Best known for: Entangling unsuspecting swimmers in deadly tentacles

Your predicament:

You're swimming in the clear, tropical waters of the Philippines. Something brushes against your leg and suddenly you're in agonizing pain.

What's the worst that can happen?

You have been stung by a box jellyfish—one of the most toxic animals in the world . . .

1. Several of the creature's long tentacles have come into contact with your legs and arms, releasing deadly poison into your bloodstream.
2. The terrible pain caused by the stings sends you into shock.
3. The poison causes your heart to fail. Then either . . .
4. You drown, or . . .
5. The poison kills you in minutes.
6. Either way, you're dead.

The good news:

You can protect yourself against the tentacles of box jellyfish by wearing a Lycra "stinger suit" or by wearing tights over any exposed flesh. The creatures are not aggressive. There is an antivenom, which is effective if given quickly.

The bad news:

More people are killed by box jellyfish than by any other sea creature. They are among the most venomous animals in the world and their poison can kill in three minutes. The pain is so extreme that it sometimes causes heart attacks. Box jellyfish are very difficult to spot and usually victims don't know the creatures are present in the water until they are stung. Most people stung by a box jellyfish die.

FIELD AGENT REPORT

How to avoid deadly jellyfish peril:

☠ If you are in an area known for box jellyfish, wear a protective suit and/or swim in a netted area (though one type, the Irukandji, is small enough to slip through the net).

If you do get stung:

☠ Apply vinegar to stings and any remaining tentacles for 30 seconds—this will neutralize the stings.

☠ After applying vinegar, remove any tentacles that are stuck to the skin—but use a cloth to do this because the tentacles can still sting even when they are detached from the jellyfish's body.

☠ Get to the hospital as soon as possible.

Fact file:

Box jellyfish (also known as sea wasps) are not really jellyfish at all: they come from a family called cubozoas. There are 19 species, two of which are capable of killing humans. The most deadly is about 10 inches in diameter and has up to 60 tentacles, which can be as long as 10 feet. The creature's toxin is released when its tentacles come into contact with chemicals on the skin of shrimps, small fish . . . and people. Contact with about 10 feet of tentacle is enough to kill an adult human. Many animals are immune to the sting, such as turtles, which eat box jellyfish. The less deadly species is smaller and can slip through protective nets, but it's much rarer for people to die from its sting.

Peril: Great White Shark

Peril rating: 6/10

Location: Most warmer seas around the world

Best known for: Vicious and very bloody attacks on surfers, swimmers, and divers

Your predicament:
After everyone else has gone home for the day, you are still surfing off the coast of Florida in pounding surf as dusk falls. The water is murky. You feel something rough against your body and realize with horror that it's a shark. It takes a bite.

What's the worst that can happen?
The shark has decided you taste good . . .

1. You look around, terrified, but can't see the shark.
2. Feeling weaker and weaker, you notice the water around you turn red.
3. Despite the fact that you've only been bitten once, the wound is very serious: this was obviously an enormous shark.
4. It comes back to finish you off.
5. You die.

The good news:
Despite the many millions of people who swim in the sea every year, on average only ten are killed by sharks. Many shark attacks do not result in death: they happen when the fish mistakes you for its usual food source (sea mammals or other fish), takes a bite, then realizes its mistake and swims off, often leaving the victim injured but alive. Your chance of surviving a shark attack is about 85%.

The bad news:
Great white sharks are huge, powerful animals with extremely sharp teeth and rough skin capable of badly grazing yours. Even if the fish only takes one bite, it could be enough to kill you. Sometimes sharks do attack people with the intention of eating them—these attacks often happen in deeper waters. Whatever the statistics, most people would agree that being eaten alive by a giant fish is a fate to be avoided at all costs.

FIELD AGENT REPORT

How to avoid deadly shark peril:

☠ Avoid swimming in places where sharks have been known to attack people. But if you do want to swim in an area where sharks are sometimes spotted . . .

☠ Avoid swimming at dusk and dawn or at night.

☠ Don't go too far out—you'll be farther away from help.

☠ Sharks are more likely to attack someone on his or her own, so swim in a group.

☠ Don't wear anything shiny—it could look like shining fish scales.

☠ Don't go into the sea if there are a lot of people fishing, either from the shore or from boats.

☠ Avoid lots of splashing around—it can attract sharks.

☠ If you are being attacked repeatedly by a shark, there's probably nothing you can do. But there have been reports of people punching sharks on the nose, causing them to swim away.

Fact file:

There are hundreds of shark species, 30 of which have been known to attack humans. Only three kinds attack people regularly: great white sharks, which reach a maximum length of 23 feet; tiger sharks, up to about 14.5 feet long; and bull sharks, which are smaller (8 feet) but known for being aggressive. Most shark attacks happen off the east coast of North America, where the majority of victims are surfers or windsurfers.

Peril: Blue-ringed Octopus

Peril rating: 8/10

Location: Australia and Japan

Best known for: Its deceptive appearance and lethal, paralyzing toxin

Your predicament:
You're snorkeling on a shallow reef in Australia. You spot a tiny yellow octopus that develops bright blue rings on its skin when you approach it. You stretch out your hand and pick it up.

What's the worst that can happen?
If you can see the creature's blue rings and you're holding it, you've probably already been bitten . . .

1. You start to feel sick.
2. Your vision becomes blurred.
3. Within seconds you can't see at all.
4. You go numb.
5. You can't speak, swallow, or breathe.
6. You die.

The good news:
The blue-ringed octopus isn't aggressive—it spends its time hiding behind rocks and in crevices. Usually, people are bitten only when they play with or pick up a blue-ringed octopus. Sometimes the octopus bites but doesn't inject venom.

The bad news:
There's enough poison in a small blue-ringed octopus's bite to kill ten adults. It's the same as the deadly poison found in fugu and it's ten thousand times stronger than cyanide. A wet suit is no protection: the octopus can bite through it. In some cases, victims may appear to be dead but in fact they are fully aware of what's going on around them. There is no antivenom.

FIELD AGENT REPORT

How to avoid deadly octopus peril:

☠ Never pick up an octopus, especially a cute little yellow or brown one (note that blue-ringed octopuses only show their blue rings when they feel threatened). Its venom takes effect so quickly that you're almost certain to die if you're on your own when bitten.

If you suspect someone else has been bitten:

☠ Call an ambulance.

☠ Start CPR.

☠ A person will survive only if treatment continues until the poison has worked its way out— which will take hours. Therefore it's essential to get the victim to the hospital ASAP.

Fact file:

There are two species of blue-ringed octopus, both found in shallow reefs and rock pools. The first species is found from northern Australia to Japan, and the second (and more common) kind is found off the coast of southern Australia. The most common species is tiny, only the size of a golf ball when fully grown, and weighs less than an ounce. The other kind measures about 8 inches with its tentacles spread out. Blue-ringed octopuses live on small crabs and fish. The poison contained in their saliva is tetrodotoxin (TTX). One milligram is enough to kill an adult.

Peril: Cone Snail

Peril rating: 5/10

Location: Indian and Pacific oceans east as far as Hawaii, north as far as Japan, and south as far as New Zealand (including all of Australia)

Best known for: Harpooning rock-poolers with its toxic tooth

Your predicament:
Paddling in a Hawaiian rock pool, you spot an interesting, brightly colored shell on the seabed and pick it up. Too late, you realize there is a creature inside it. Before you can put it down, a fierce pain shoots up your arm.

What's the worst that can happen?
You have been stung by a large cone snail and, unfortunately for you, this is a particularly dangerous species, the kind that lives on fish . . .

1. You feel intense pain.
2. Your hand and arm swell and become tingly and numb.
3. You feel sick and your muscles become paralyzed.
4. Your vision is blurred.
5. The poison causes you to stop breathing.
6. You die.

The good news:
You won't be stung by a cone snail unless you pick it up. There have only ever been a few recorded deaths. Many of the smaller species' stings are not very dangerous.

The bad news:
There is no antivenom. The snail's harpoonlike tooth can inject its poison through the shells of other mollusks—so it can also sting through a wet suit. The poison can act quickly—one species is said to kill within about ten minutes. The attractive markings on cone snails' shells mean people are likely to pick them up.

FIELD AGENT REPORT

How to avoid deadly cone snail peril:

☠ Never handle shells in tropical waters unless you're absolutely sure there are no animals inside them.

☠ If you are stung by a cone snail, get to a hospital as quickly as possible. The only treatment is providing life support until the poison has been processed by the victim's body.

Fact file:

Cone snails are sea snails, of which there are many species. They live in cone-shaped shells that are often patterned and/or brightly colored. The larger species can grow up to 8 inches long. They eat worms, mollusks, and small fish. Most types of cone snail are not very dangerous to humans, but the species that live on fish have the strongest poison because they move slowly but need to stop fast-swimming fish. Two species have been known to kill people.

Peril: Piranha

Peril rating: 4/10

Location: Lakes and rivers in South America, from Argentina to Colombia, and occasionally the U.S.

Best known for: Stripping the flesh from large mammals in a matter of seconds

Your predicament:

You're on a riverbank in South America and notice a large pool left behind by heavy rainfall. It's hot and you decide to take a dip. You notice a shoal of shiny fish in the water.

What's the worst that can happen?

If the fish are piranhas and are especially hungry . . .

1. A hungry fish bites, taking a big chunk out of your flesh.
2. Another half-starved fish in the shoal does the same and the scent of blood in the water attracts others.
3. You die of shock or a heart attack.
4. The fish eat you.

The good news:

It's true that shoals of piranhas can be dangerous when very hungry, but more often than not they will leave human beings alone. Usually a piranha fish will take just one bite—which admittedly can be rather nasty and might result in an amputated toe or finger. But where there have been reported cases of piranhas eating human flesh, it's very likely that the victims drowned first.

The bad news:

Piranha fish have strong jaws and sharp teeth that interlock and can inflict a serious bite. They are attracted by the presence of blood in the water. Piranhas are often grouped together in large shoals.

FIELD AGENT REPORT

How to avoid deadly piranha peril:

☠ Keep away from pools left after a flood, where piranhas may have become trapped and are starving.

☠ Avoid water near nesting birds or garbage dumps (both of which are potential piranha snack bars).

☠ Don't enter the water if you have a cut or sore—piranhas (and other animals) can sense blood in the water.

☠ Keep your movements as calm as possible.

☠ Remember that piranhas are only active during the day (though plenty of other dangerous creatures are active at night!).

Fact file:

Piranha fish are especially common in the Amazon River. Red-bellied piranha are the most ferocious, have the sharpest teeth and strongest jaws, and reach up to 13 inches in length. They live on insects, fish, worms, and small mammals and birds that fall into the water. Some piranha species feed on little bites taken from the fins and scales of other fish. Other species are vegetarian and use their sharp teeth to crack nuts that fall into the water.

Peril: Electric Eel

Peril rating: 3/10

Location: Amazon and Orinoco rivers of South America

Best known for: High-voltage attacks

Your predicament:

You're fishing in sluggish, shallow waters of the Orinoco River in Venezuela. As you wade into the water to retrieve a fish, you are suddenly knocked off your feet by a powerful force.

What's the worst that can happen?

You have received a strong electrical shock from a large electric eel . . .

1. You stagger backward, straight into the path of the escaping eel.
2. The eel shocks you again.
3. You fall into the river, stunned.
4. Unable to get up, you drown in shallow water.

The good news:

Electric eels are not aggressive creatures and shock large animals only in self-defense. One shock is not enough to kill a human: you would need to be shocked several times. The eel wants to get away, not eat you—it doesn't even have teeth. The creatures are nocturnal. Human deaths from encounters with electric eels are extremely rare.

The bad news:

Electric eels can deliver a shock up to 650 volts (a U.S. electrical socket traditionally carries 120 volts). They can even emit an electrical charge up to eight hours after their death, making them potential hazards if they are caught in fishing nets.

FIELD AGENT REPORT

How to avoid deadly electric eel peril:

☠ Don't wade into slow-moving rivers and swamps in South America: electric eels are fairly common in these waters, along with plenty of other creatures you probably don't want to meet.

☠ If you do find yourself wading in these rivers, don't do so alone.

☠ Wear rubber boots and carry a wooden stick, which can be used to check the water in front of you.

Fact file:

Electric eels look like eels but are more closely related to catfish. They can reach up to 8 feet in length and weigh up to 44 pounds. The organs used for electrical discharge take up most of the creature's body. Electric eels use their electrical charge to kill fish and other small prey, and to deter large predators. After delivering an especially big shock, the eel needs time to recharge its batteries (this happens in the fish's metabolism—they don't need to be plugged in). They also use their electrical receptors to detect other fish.

Peril: **Stonefish**

Peril rating: 7/10

Location: Tropical shallow waters and coral reefs

Best known for: Spearing swimmers' feet with jagged, highly poisonous spines

Your predicament:
You're swimming alone, close to a coral reef in the Red Sea, off the coast of Egypt. The water is shallow and you stand up to rest on some light-colored rocks. As you put your feet on the seabed, a terrible pain shoots through your foot.

What's the worst that can happen?
You have stepped on a stonefish, the most venomous fish in the world . . .

1. Spines on the stonefish's back penetrate deep into your foot.
2. Venom shoots up the spines and deep into the wound.
3. You are in terrible pain and go into shock.
4. Your foot quickly becomes very swollen.
5. You feel weak and unable to move.
6. Unable to get to a hospital by yourself, you die.

The good news:
Although the stonefish is the world's most venomous fish, it doesn't always kill—if only a few of the spines have penetrated your foot, or if they haven't gone in very deep, you have a good chance of survival. The fish isn't aggressive. There is an antivenom.

The bad news:
Stonefish are well camouflaged (as their name suggests). The venom causes intense pain and can kill a human being in two hours, so if you are in a remote area or alone, you're at greater risk. Stonefish can live out of water for up to 12 hours: people have been killed by them while walking along the beach, yards away from the sea, at low tide. Stonefish kill more people than sharks do.

FIELD AGENT REPORT

How to avoid deadly stonefish peril:

☠ Be very careful where you put your feet in tropical waters.

☠ Shuffle, don't walk, into the sea from the beach to reduce the chance of stepping on a stonefish (or other creatures).

☠ Wear thick-soled beach shoes—though even then a stonefish's spines may penetrate.

☠ Don't go swimming or snorkeling alone.

If you are stung by a stonefish:

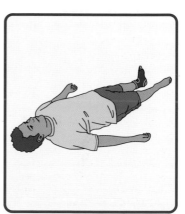

☠ Get to the hospital immediately, where you will be given antivenom.

☠ In the meantime, a hot compress can relieve the pain. Don't try to restrict the movement of the poison.

Fact file:
There are two species of stonefish, also known as goblinfish and warty ghouls. The fish are usually brown in color, sometimes with red markings to blend in with surroundings, and bumpy, warty-looking skin.

Peril: Stingray

Peril rating: 4/10

Location: Tropical and temperate waters worldwide

Best known for: Lurking camouflaged on the seabed, ready to deploy its deadly stinger

Your predicament:
You're swimming in shallow water close to the beach in the Caribbean when suddenly you feel a searing pain in your chest. There's a cloud of sand beneath you and, as you struggle for breath, you see a stingray swimming away.

What's the worst that can happen?
You were swimming directly above a large stingray, which became alarmed and raised its whip-like tail . . .

1. The stingray's barbed stinger has become embedded in your chest.
2. You are in terrible pain due to the wound and the stingray's venom.
3. Unfortunately, the stinger has become embedded in a vital organ.
4. You die.

The good news:
Stingrays are not aggressive creatures and sting only in self-defense (though there is some argument about this and there have been a few reports of possible aggressive behavior). The venom is not usually deadly unless the stinger becomes lodged in the chest or abdomen. Deaths from stingray strikes are extremely rare. Most stingray injuries to humans are to the legs and feet, when a stingray is disturbed by someone walking into the sea from the beach, and they're not usually life-threatening.

The bad news:
It can be very difficult to spot stingrays when they are buried under sand—you may not realize they are there and swim too close—and the venom is extremely painful. The barbed stinger is very hard to remove. A strike can be fatal if it hits a vital organ.

FIELD AGENT REPORT

How to avoid deadly stingray peril:

☠ Shuffle slowly into the sea so that any rays will be alerted to your presence and swim away.

☠ If you see one, swim away from it and definitely not directly above it.

☠ Never try to touch or catch a stingray.

If you are stung:

☠ Get to the hospital as soon as you can—you may need a local anesthetic, a course of antibiotics, and an X-ray for pieces of barb or spine lodged in the wound.

☠ In the meantime, immerse the wound in very hot water (as hot as you can stand) or apply a very hot compress—this will reduce the pain. Keep applying heat for 30–90 minutes.

Fact file:
Stingrays are flat fish related to sharks. There are numerous species, found in fresh and sea water in many different parts of the world. They vary in size from just a few inches to several feet long. They have a long tail with a nail-like stinger in it, which can be up to 14 inches long.

Peril: Sea Snake

Peril rating: 4/10

Location: Warmer seas, mainly in the Pacific and Indian oceans

Best known for: Darting through the water to envenom swimmers with its deadly fangs

Your predicament:

You're swimming in Thailand and spot a striped snake in the water. It seems unaggressive, and you've heard that sea snakes' fangs are short and point backward, making them incapable of biting a human being. So, playfully, you grab the snake's tail—it bites you and swims off.

What's the worst that can happen?

You have been bitten by a faint-banded sea snake, one of the most venomous sea snakes in the world . . .

1. Ten minutes after being bitten, you start to ache and feel weak.
2. As you try to swim back to shore, you feel sick and start to vomit.
3. You make it back to shore, aching all over.
4. Your muscles become paralyzed and you struggle for breath as the muscles that control breathing are affected.
5. Without medical attention, you die from respiratory failure.

The good news:

There is an antivenom. Around 90% of bites from sea snakes are "dry bites"— they don't inject venom. The bite itself is not very painful. If the snake does inject poison, it may not be enough to kill you. Sea snakes only bite if provoked. Fishermen often find sea snakes caught in fishing nets and throw them back into the sea with their bare hands without being bitten. Although they are more poisonous than land snakes, sea snakes cause fewer deaths.

The bad news:

Despite the myths, sea snakes are capable of biting humans. A full bite from a sea snake that injects sufficient venom is enough to kill an adult human being. Because sea snake venom destroys muscle tissue, even if victims do survive they can suffer severe kidney problems. They are the most numerous and widespread group of venomous reptiles in the world.

FIELD AGENT REPORT

How to avoid deadly sea snake peril:

☠ You have to be either foolish or unlucky to be bitten by a sea snake. If one approaches you, remain calm—it won't attack you unless you attack it.

If you are bitten:

☠ Get to the hospital as soon as possible for antivenom and other medical treatment.

☠ In the meantime, apply a pressure bandage to the bite area, as far up the limb as possible, and keep it still.

Fact file:

Sea snakes look like land snakes but with a flattened tail that acts as a rudder. There are two separate groups—true sea snakes and the nocturnal sea kraits. All are venomous. The faint-banded sea snake is one of the most venomous, along with the Dubois. Most adult sea snakes are 3.5 to 5 feet long; sea kraits tend to be a little smaller. Most species like shallow waters less than 100 feet deep; some species prefer coral reefs, while others prefer muddy or sandy seabeds. Sea snakes can swim up rivers several miles from the ocean. They live on fish and eels. They breathe air but can stay underwater for hours.

Land Snake

Sea Snake

Sea Krait

Peril: Giant Squid

Peril rating: 1/10

Location: Deep seas all over the world, though uncommon in tropical and polar regions

Best known for: Clambering on board ships and dragging sailors to a horrible death in the darkest ocean depths

Your predicament:
You're scuba diving off the west coast of Scotland, exploring a shipwreck on the seabed. Suddenly you spot something: could it have been an enormous tentacle disappearing behind the wrecked ship's hull?

What's the worst that can happen?
You swim over to have a closer look . . .

1. A 30-foot-long squid swims toward you at an alarming speed. Before you can swim to safety, you are trapped by two enormous tentacles.
2. You struggle but are painfully gripped by the creature's powerful suckers.
3. Your air tank becomes detached.
4. The squid brings you toward its beak.
5. Mercifully, you drown before the squid can eat you alive.

The good news:
No one has ever actually been killed by a giant squid, at least as far as we know. They live at depths of more than 650 feet below sea level, so you would be unlikely to see one on a recreational dive. In fact, few people have ever seen a live giant squid, despite the fact that many people have made a point of looking for them.

The bad news:
Giant squid fight sperm whales and sometimes win (dead sperm whales have been found with giant sucker scars on their skin). They are equipped with long tentacles, each covered in suckers that contain gripping teeth, and a sharp beak like a parrot's but about the size of a grapefruit. A giant squid could easily kill a human being. If you're worried about large squid, there's an even bigger one: the colossal squid. You're much more likely to encounter Humboldt squid, which are not so big but have been known to attack people.

FIELD AGENT REPORT

How to avoid deadly giant squid peril:

☠ Avoid diving at depths greater than 650 feet.

☠ Not much is known about giant squid, but judging by other types of squid you should be alarmed if it lights up in any way (other species use bioluminescence to confuse their prey).

☠ If the squid swims at you with two tentacles extended toward you, do anything you can to make your escape.

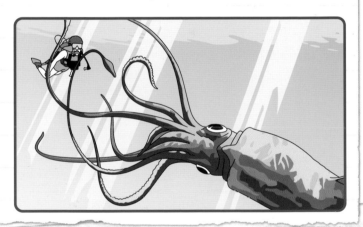

Fact file:

Giant squid are thought to live at depths of up to 1,100 yards in temperate oceans worldwide. Only recently have live giant squid begun to be scientifically studied—before 2004 the creatures were only known from dead ones that had been washed up, a few caught in nets, and remains found in the stomachs of sperm whales. Giant squid have eight arms, plus two extra tentacles that they use to catch their prey, all covered in teeth-filled suckers. They grow up to about 33 feet long, though the largest giant squid ever recorded was 61 feet, found near New Zealand in 1880. The eyes of giant squid are bigger than a human head.

DEADLY PLANET

Planet Earth can do some very
alarming things, like erupting,
shaking violently, or shooting
spumes of boiling water into
the air. As staying indoors
isn't generally the best defense,
it would be wise to read this
section without further delay.

Peril: Volcano

Peril rating: 7/10

Location: Worldwide

Best known for: Spewing out lethal, red-hot lava, ash, and toxic gases

Your predicament:

You're on vacation in Sicily, hiking on the slopes of Mount Etna. The ground shakes in a series of small earthquakes. Suddenly you hear a rumbling sound that quickly builds to a huge explosion.

What's the worst that can happen?

Unfortunately for you, you chose the wrong day for a hike . . .

1. After the initial eruption, an enormous pyroclastic flow (hot toxic gas and pieces of dust and rock) moves down the mountainside at 60 mph.
2. You heed warnings to find shelter and a filter to breathe through.
3. You're directly in the path of the flow, which blasts away the building you're in before vaporizing you.
4. You die.

The good news:

Not all volcanic eruptions involve pyroclastic flows. Lava flows are usually slow enough for people to get out of the way, and the lava doesn't cover a very large area. Scientists are becoming better and better at predicting when volcanoes will erupt, which means the area can be evacuated beforehand.

The bad news:

Lava is extremely hot—between 1,300° and 2,370° F—and can explode if it comes into contact with water or vegetation. Ash from a volcano can be more hazardous than lava, often covering a larger area with a thick, choking layer. Most dangerous of all, pyroclastic flows can reach temperatures of over 1,470° F and speeds of over 90 mph. Volcanoes can also cause landslides and the release of deadly gases, both of which may be more dangerous than the eruption itself.

FIELD AGENT REPORT

How to avoid deadly volcano peril:

 If you live near a volcano, you should have an emergency kit ready, including water, canned food, dust masks, radio, blankets, a flashlight, etc.

 Stay indoors, unless told to evacuate, and move to a higher floor.

 If a pyroclastic flow is heading your way, cover your nose and mouth and don't breathe as the flow passes.

Pyroclastic Flow

 Follow any evacuation advice immediately.

Fact file:

A volcano is a mountain sitting on top of a pool of molten rock called magma. As pressure builds up, magma escapes through an opening in the mountain. Magma that reaches the surface is called lava. Most volcanoes are on plate boundaries in the Earth's crust. Mount Etna is Europe's biggest volcano (almost 11,000 feet high) and one of the most active in the world. There are more than 500 active volcanoes on Earth, many of which are under the sea. Scientists monitor volcanoes by checking the gases they release, changes to their structure, and nearby small earthquakes.

Peril: **Whirlpool**

Peril rating: 3/10

Location: Worldwide

Best known for: Dragging ships down into an inescapable vortex

Your predicament:
You're on a small tourist boat visiting the famous Naruto whirlpool in Japanese waters. The boat draws close enough for you to take a good picture . . .

What's the worst that can happen?
The inboard engine splutters dramatically, then stops . . .

1. Strong currents rock the boat and pull it into the huge whirlpool.
2. You lose your balance and tumble overboard.
3. The foaming water drags you to the center at speeds of 13 mph.
4. You are sucked down into the vortex.
5. You drown.

The good news:
Unless you decide to go for a dip in a whirlpool, or take a small boat into one, you should be fine: whirlpools are not usually strong enough to overturn a large boat. Dangerous whirlpools are rare.

The bad news:
Some whirlpools are powerful and have a strong downward pull as well as spin. If you swim or canoe near a strong whirlpool, you could easily drown.

FIELD AGENT REPORT

How to avoid deadly whirlpool peril:

☠ Don't swim, dive, or take a small boat or canoe anywhere near a whirlpool.

☠ Even large boats and ships need to be aware of whirlpools and take note of especially dangerous times, such as during flood tides.

☠ A combination of tide and currents, especially close to large rocks in the sea, can create dangerous whirlpools.

☠ If you are caught in a whirlpool, paddle toward the edge and hope it's not too strong.

Fact file:

Whirlpools are caused by fast-moving tides or currents that cause the water to spin around violently, often forming a vortex (downward pull). The vortex of the Naruto whirlpool can be 65 feet in diameter. The Naruto is one of the world's five strongest whirlpools: the others are Old Sow, off the coast of New Brunswick, Canada, which is also the largest at 82 yards in diameter; the Corryvreckan in Scotland; the Saltstraumen near Bodo in Norway (the fastest, with speeds of 23 mph); and the Moskstraumen, near the Lofoten Islands in Norway—this whirlpool is also known as the Maelstrom, which is another name for a whirlpool. There are smaller whirlpools all over the world that can also be dangerous.

Peril: Avalanche

Peril rating: 7/10

Location: Mountains worldwide

Best known for: Sweeping skiers from mountainsides and burying them deep in the snow

Your predicament:

You're snowboarding on a steep ski slope. There's been a lot of heavy snow recently and it's windy. You notice some cracks in the snow. You hear a thunking sound.

What's the worst that can happen?

These signs make it very likely that within the next few seconds you'll be caught in an avalanche . . .

1. The top layer of snow you're standing on fractures and starts to slide, taking you with it.
2. You hurtle downhill at 60 mph as the avalanche picks up speed.
3. When the avalanche eventually stops, you're buried under yards of snow.
4. The snow sets hard around you and you're unable to breathe.
5. You die.

The good news:

It's rare for an avalanche to happen without warning, so you can look for signs and take precautions to increase your chances of survival. Most people who are caught in an avalanche survive.

The bad news:

After an avalanche, the snow sets as hard as cement within seconds, making it impossible to move or breathe. You won't be able to dig yourself out once the avalanche has stopped, unless you're very near the surface. It's also extremely difficult to control what happens to you in an avalanche, so you can be flung against trees or rocks or off a precipice.

FIELD AGENT REPORT

How to avoid deadly avalanche peril:

☠ Always check avalanche reports before leaving for the slopes, and learn the danger signs for yourself.

If you are caught in an avalanche:

☠ Discard skis but hold on to a ski pole.

☠ Don't cry out or open your mouth during the avalanche.

☠ Use swimming motions to try to stay near the surface of the snow.

☠ Put your hands in front of your face and try to make an air space as the avalanche draws to a stop.

☠ Always carry your phone and an avalanche beacon (or "transceiver"), which will tell rescuers where you are.

☠ If you end up near the surface, try to poke out your ski pole so that rescuers can find you quickly.

☠ Only shout out when you think a rescuer is nearby.

Fact file:

There are two main types of avalanches: a loose snow avalanche is a cascade of powdery snow and isn't usually dangerous; a slab avalanche is when a large plate-like chunk of heavy snow breaks away from a weaker layer of snow underneath it. This type of avalanche is much more dangerous. Over 90% of avalanches are caused by the weight of a person or snowmobile on unstable snow. A large avalanche might consist of 330,000 cubic yards of snow and travel at 80 mph.

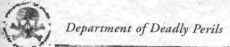

Peril: Forest Fire

Peril rating: 5/10

Location: Worldwide

Best known for: Raging uncontrolled, leaving death and devastation in its wake

Your predicament:

You're hiking in a Washington state pine forest when you smell burning—you assume it's a campfire. You notice a wisp of smoke in the distance, but think nothing of it. An hour later, you notice more smoke in a line ahead of you. You decide to turn back.

What's the worst that can happen?

A raging forest fire is creeping ever closer . . .

1. You try to run away, moving uphill.
2. You start to see burning embers blown around in the wind.
3. You run as fast as you can across a large field of dry grass.
4. You are overtaken by a 10-feet-tall fire traveling at more than 18 mph.
5. You die.

The good news:

You should be able to spot the signs that a forest fire is likely. Emergency services will be trying to contain the fire and rescue anyone caught in its path. There are tactics you can use to increase your chances of survival.

The bad news:

Forest fires are common and can move faster than you can run. Smaller fires outside the main one can block your route. Fire can jump roads and other bare areas—even streams. The wind can carry embers a mile from the main fire to start smaller ones in your line of flight. Wild animals will be moving away from the fire as well and may present an extra danger.

FIELD AGENT REPORT

How to avoid deadly forest fire peril:

☠ If you go hiking after a period of drought, stay alert for a burning smell, or fine particles of ash carried on the wind.

☠ If you are trapped, your best chance of survival is to move to the middle of an area with little vegetation—a road, water, a plowed field, or rocks, for example.

☠ If you are in water, move to the middle and try to keep as much of your body beneath the surface as possible.

☠ Cover any exposed skin.

☠ Once the fire has passed, make your getaway across the area the fire has already burned.

☠ Move downwind and to lower ground: fires travel faster uphill than downhill.

☠ If you're in a car, stay in it. The extra protection outweighs the risk that the fuel tank could explode. Lie on the floor and take shallow breaths.

☠ If all else fails, find a ditch, lie in it, cover yourself with as much earth as possible, and wait for the fire to pass.

Fact file:

Forest fires are most common in the summer and autumn. They are often the result of negligence—e.g., campfires that haven't been put out properly—and can also be caused by lightning. Some ecosystems around the world have evolved to take advantage of forest fires—seeds germinate in very high temperatures.

Peril: Tsunami

Peril rating: 7/10

Location: Low-lying coastal areas worldwide, but especially in the Pacific

Best known for: Laying waste to coastal towns and villages

Your predicament:

You're on vacation on the Tonga Islands in the Pacific Ocean. You feel the ground shake slightly.

What's the worst that can happen?

The tremors you felt were caused by an undersea earthquake, which has triggered a tsunami . . .

1. You're on the beach when you notice the sea drawing back to an unusual distance from the shore.
2. You stay by the beach, looking at the recently uncovered sea life.
3. You notice a large wave heading toward you—it doesn't look particularly dangerous.
4. The wave is a lot more powerful than it looks. It picks you up and sweeps you inland.
5. You are struck by various pieces of debris.
6. You die.

The good news:

A sudden drawback of the sea, exposing areas of seabed usually underwater, can be a sign a tsunami is on its way—this can give people time to run for high ground. In some areas, special coastal barriers minimize damage. In the Pacific, the Tsunami Warning System monitors earthquakes and issues tsunami warnings based on expert knowledge of undersea quakes.

The bad news:

Tsunamis are difficult to predict, and often ships don't notice them because in deep water the waves are not high. The sea will rush in much faster than you can run. There is usually a series of waves, and the first isn't necessarily the most dangerous. Tsunamis can be as high as 100 feet. The retreating water before a tsunami can sweep people out to sea. Heavy rocks can be flung inland and whole buildings destroyed—you are in danger of being hit by debris.

FIELD AGENT REPORT

How to avoid deadly tsunami peril:

☠ If you see the water receding from shore very rapidly, this may give you up to five minutes to run to safety.

☠ Don't stay inside if you are in a small building.

☠ If you have some warning, head for high ground or a sturdy, tall building.

☠ Don't leave a safe area after one wave has hit—there will probably be more, and subsequent waves may be more dangerous than the first.

☠ If you feel an earthquake, it's better to stay away from the beach and find somewhere safe inland on higher ground, even if there isn't a tsunami warning.

☠ If you're in a boat, don't return to shore until you hear it's safe to do so.

Fact file:

Tsunamis are also known as tidal waves, but have nothing to do with tides: they are most often caused by earthquakes under the sea. Landslides, underwater volcanoes and other underwater explosions, and (very rarely) meteorites can also cause a tsunami. Eighty percent of tsunamis happen in the Pacific Ocean. The waves move fast in deep water (up to 500 mph), but are not very high. As the waves make their way to shore and the water becomes shallower, they slow down and increase in height.

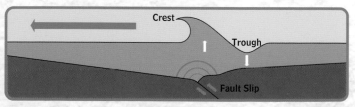

Peril: **Quicksand**

Peril rating: 2/10

Location: Worldwide

Best known for: Sucking hapless hikers to a slow and horrible death in a bottomless pit

Your predicament:
You're walking along a riverbank in remote Scottish moorland, when suddenly—*squelch*—you fall into a patch of quicksand.

What's the worst that can happen?
You start to panic . . .

1. You sink into the quicksand and can't feel the bottom.
2. You begin screaming and flailing your arms and legs.
3. You become short of breath and can't reach solid ground.
4. You sink lower and start to swallow the quicksand.
5. You drown.

The good news:
Despite what you might have seen at the movies, quicksand CANNOT suck you down—in fact, it's easier to float in quicksand than in ordinary water. As long as you're not wearing very heavy gear, you'll be able to float and reach the side. It's very unusual for quicksand to be so deep that you can't touch the bottom (despite the myths about bottomless pits).

The bad news:
Quicksand is found all over the world and in all sorts of places—riverbanks and dry riverbeds, hilly country, beaches—and is often very difficult to spot.

FIELD AGENT REPORT

How to avoid deadly quicksand peril:

☠ Carry a stick to test the ground. If you're very eagle-eyed, you can recognize patches of quicksand because they look different from the ground around them.

☠ If you feel the ground beneath your feet becoming boggy, move back to more solid ground.

If you do fall into a patch of quicksand:

☠ Take off anything heavy you're wearing, like a backpack.

☠ If the quicksand is shallow enough for you to stand up, take very slow steps backward until you reach the edge. If the quicksand is above your thighs or you can't feel the bottom, lie back and float faceup, then swim to the side using slow movements.

Fact file:

Quicksand is sand, silt, or clay that is so saturated with water that it has become liquid. Often it will look just like ordinary sand, but heavy objects will sink into it. Quicksand is usually made by underground springs pushing water upward into the sand or silt. It can also be formed by vibration (for example, from an earthquake) that causes the grains of sand to move quickly from side to side, though this is much less common.

Peril: Earthquake

Peril rating: 7/10

Location: Worldwide

Best known for: Toppling buildings, opening great chasms in the earth, destroying entire cities

Your predicament:
You're in a hotel reception area in the center of Tokyo when you feel the ground begin to shake.

What's the worst that can happen?
As the seconds pass, the shaking becomes more intense . . .

1. Panic-stricken, you feel you have to get out of the hotel to avoid being buried beneath the building.
2. Ignoring everyone's advice, you run out into the street.
3. The ground is shaking violently and you see a split open up in the road ahead of you.
4. You are hit on the head by a potted begonia falling from the fourth story of a building.
5. You die.

The good news:
Most earthquakes are very small. Even if you experience a large earthquake, the chances of survival are good. Building materials and techniques are improving all the time and ever safer structures are being built in earthquake-prone areas such as Japan and California.

The bad news:
Big earthquakes can be immensely destructive: falling objects, toppled buildings, broken power lines, and cracks in the earth all present serious hazards. Predicting earthquakes is very difficult. There are usually between 10 and 20 major earthquakes every year around the planet. Nowhere in the world is entirely free from the risk of earthquakes.

FIELD AGENT REPORT

How to avoid deadly earthquake peril:

If an earthquake starts when you're indoors:

☠ Stay there—you're safer than outside.

☠ Crouch in a corner, or underneath a sturdy table, with your arms covering your head.

☠ Avoid windows and any high objects that might fall and hit you.

If you're outside:

☠ Keep away from buildings and trees. Lie on the ground with your head covered.

☠ If you're in a car, stop it somewhere away from buildings, bridges, and trees and stay inside it.

Fact file:

The Earth's crust is made up of enormous plates that are constantly moving. Earthquakes are caused when two plates grind against each other until eventually one of them gives way. Most earthquakes aren't strong enough to cause any damage. More than a million happen every year, most around the rim of the Pacific Ocean—the "Ring of Fire." Earthquakes can have foreshocks, but unfortunately it's impossible to tell whether or not the smaller earthquakes herald a bigger one. After the main earthquake there can be aftershocks, which can continue for a long time.

Peril: Rip Current

Peril rating: 4/10

Location: Worldwide

Best known for: Pulling swimmers out to sea and drowning them

Your predicament:
You're swimming close to Ocean Beach in San Francisco, California, an area of shoreline notorious for its rip currents.

What's the worst that can happen?
After a while, you realize you are much farther out to sea than you thought . . .

1. You swim a few strokes back toward the beach but you are only pulled farther out to sea by the current.
2. You panic, struggling to head for the shore.
3. The current is strong and it isn't long before you get tired.
4. Gradually, you become unable to fight the current.
5. You are exhausted as the current pulls you out to sea.
6. You drown.

The good news:
In tourist spots, beaches with dangerous currents are well signposted and often have flags flying to indicate a safe area to swim in. If you do get pulled out to sea by a current, you have a good chance of survival as long as you don't panic. The currents do not drag people underwater but out to sea—they only extend as far as the surf zone.

The bad news:
Even the strongest swimmer can drown in a rip current. Conditions that indicate rip currents are often difficult to spot, and they can be unpredictable. According to the U.S. Life Saving Association, 80% of lifeguard rescues are due to rip currents. Rip currents can extend 440 yards out into the ocean in some areas. Currents can reach speeds of up to 6 mph—faster even than an Olympic swimmer.

FIELD AGENT REPORT

How to avoid deadly rip current peril:

☠ Always take note of any beach warnings.

☠ Currents are difficult to spot, but you can look out for signs such as broken wave patterns.

If you are taken out to sea by a current:

☠ Don't panic.

☠ Swim parallel to the shore. Don't try to swim back to shore against the current—if you do this you'll quickly become tired and could drown.

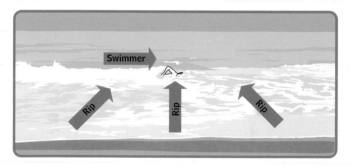

☠ Once you're free of the current, you can swim back into shore, or let the waves bring you in.

Fact file:

Rip currents are caused by waves hitting the beach in such a way that water is deflected rapidly back out to sea, and they often occur where there is an underwater sandbar. They have nothing to do with tides, which are not usually very strong.

Peril: Geyser

Peril rating: 4/10

Location: Parts of the United States, Chile, Iceland, Russia, Alaska, and New Zealand

Best known for: Exploding in a lethal jet of hot steam

Your predicament:
You're in the Rotorua–Taupo region of New Zealand, famous for its geysers and bubbling mud pools. You are on a guided tour but want to take a closer look.

What's the worst that can happen?
Unwisely, and despite warnings not to, you step off the boardwalk and approach the geyser . . .

1. You don't realize that in fact the ground here is just a very thin crust.
2. You plunge into superheated water.
3. You die.

The good news:
The world's few geysers and hot springs are tourist attractions and have plenty of signs. If you obey the safety instructions, you shouldn't be in any danger.

The bad news:
Water that erupts from geysers can be hundreds of degrees Fahrenheit. In geothermal areas the ground may be a thin crust incapable of supporting your weight, even though it can look perfectly safe and may have grass or other vegetation growing on it. People have died at geysers and hot pools, even in recent years, despite the warnings to tourists in geothermal areas. It's possible to access areas of geothermal activity that aren't marked with signs and boardwalks.

FIELD AGENT REPORT

How to avoid deadly geyser peril:

☠ Remember that geysers are extremely hot and potentially lethal—take note of all warnings and safety instructions.

☠ Stay on boardwalks and don't run on them.

☠ Never try to touch the water—it may be scalding, and you could also fall in.

☠ If you are in an area where there are no boardwalks, don't go close to the edge of a pool, as there may be an overhang.

☠ Never enter a thermal area without a guide who knows the area, and definitely don't go alone.

Fact file:

There are about a thousand active geysers in the world, half of them in Yellowstone National Park. Geysers are formed where rainwater collects deep underground in cracks in the rock and is heated by volcanic activity: the boiling water forces its way up and out of a narrow opening in the surface. Most geysers last a few minutes, then stop and start again at intervals. For example, Old Faithful in Yellowstone National Park erupts once an hour, spewing out 15 gallons of water with each eruption. The largest geyser at Rotorua–Taupo regularly erupts at 50–60 feet high.

Peril: Waterfalls

Peril rating: 5/10

Location: Worldwide

Best known for: Sweeping hapless swimmers over rocky precipices

Your predicament:
You are hiking in Yosemite National Park in California. Near the top of one of its waterfalls, Vernal Fall, you can't resist a dip in the calm-looking waters of Emerald Pool.

What's the worst that can happen?
The pool feels as refreshing as it looked. But as you move out into the water you feel the tug of a strong current . . .

1. The current pulls you underwater and drags you toward the towering precipice, previously obscured by vegetation.
2. You plunge over the waterfall headfirst, bashing different parts of your body against jagged rocks as you do so.
3. You die.

The good news:
There are lots of warning signs at Vernal Fall, and this is true of most waterfalls that are tourist attractions. It should be obvious that swimming anywhere near the top of a waterfall is likely to place you in deadly peril.

The bad news:
Pools at the tops of waterfalls often look calm but have very strong currents that drag you underwater and over the waterfall. Waterfalls do not have to be especially tall to present a serious risk: people have died being swept over waterfalls only a few yards high, because they have banged their heads on rocks.

FIELD AGENT REPORT

How to avoid deadly waterfall peril:

☠ Don't swim anywhere near the top of a waterfall—currents can easily drag you 100 yards or more.

If you are swept over a waterfall:

☠ Take a deep breath and try to jump as far away from the edge as you can.

☠ Make sure you fall feet first.

☠ Start swimming as soon as you hit the water at the bottom, ensuring you reach the surface to take in oxygen as soon as possible.

Fact file:

Waterfalls are rivers plunging over cliffs or ledges of hard rock, and are found all around the world. Vernal Fall is 110 yards high, nowhere near the world's tallest: the highest waterfall on earth, at 1,070 yards, is Angel Falls in Venezuela. Norway has five of the world's ten highest waterfalls. Every year, at least one person is swept over one of the waterfalls in Yosemite National Park, and around the world there are hundreds of waterfall deaths per year.

Vernal Fall	Angel Falls	Yosemite National Park

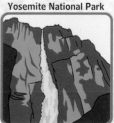

Peril: **Landslide**

Peril rating: 6/10

Location: Mountains and steep hills worldwide

Best known for: Crashing down mountainsides in a surge of destruction

Your predicament:

You're in the Philippines, where more than 90% of the country's original forest has disappeared because of logging in the last hundred years. You are staying in a town by the sea, close to the foot of a steep hill. There has been unusually heavy rainfall recently. Looking up you notice soil trickling downhill, and a tree seems to be off-center.

What's the worst that can happen?

You feel concerned by the signs you've noticed—and you're right to be . . .

1. You hear a crashing sound and look up the hill to see a mountain of mud along with several buildings hurtling toward you.
2. As you run to try and escape the landslide, the ground beneath your feet gives way.
3. The entire hillside plummets down toward the sea, taking buildings with it and covering everything, including you, in deep mud.
4. You die.

The good news:

Most landslides are quite small and don't occur in populated areas. It's possible to survive a landslide—even a serious one.

The bad news:

Depending on the speed of the landslide, you may not have time to take any action at all. Major landslides can kill hundreds or even thousands of people.

FIELD AGENT REPORT

How to avoid deadly landslide peril:

☠ If you live in an area prone to landslides, keep an eye out for warning signs such as muddy rivers, especially if there is increased rainfall.

☠ Be prepared to evacuate.

If you are caught in a landslide:

☠ Get out of the direct path of the landslide if possible.

☠ If not, curl into a ball and put your arms over your head.

☠ If you're indoors, find a strong table and take shelter under it.

☠ If you're outside, find something big and sturdy, like a large rock, to stay behind.

Fact file:

In a landslide, a layer of soil and sediment becomes separated from the rock underneath and moves downhill—sometimes at speeds of over 125 mph. They can be caused by many different factors: heavy rainfall or snow melt, earthquakes and volcanoes and erosion, and human activity such as deforestation or mining. The largest landslide in history happened in 1980 at Mount St. Helen's in the United States: it was triggered by a volcano and rushed downhill at 150 mph. Landslides can sometimes cause tsunamis.

Peril: Desert

Peril rating: 7/10

Location: Worldwide

Best known for: Being the most inhospitable terrain on the planet

Your predicament:
You are exploring Australia's Great Sandy Desert by jeep and decide to visit a remote meteorite site. You have driven off-road for some distance when your jeep becomes stuck in a sand dune.

What's the worst that can happen?
You try to call for help, but your phone has run out of battery. After many long hours attempting to move the jeep, you decide to abandon it and walk in search of civilization . . .

1. You don't have much water with you and have no idea how to find any. You try to conserve it, but it soon runs out.
2. In the strong heat of the desert you start to suffer from heat exhaustion, with headache, dizziness, fatigue, and stomach cramps.
3. You develop heatstroke—as well as the symptoms of heat exhaustion. You start to feel disoriented and confused. You have hallucinations.
4. With no way of getting water, you lie down and lose consciousness.
5. You die.

The good news:
People have lived in the Australian outback for thousands of years, so it is possible to survive there if you have some local knowledge and survival techniques. If you prepare well before you set off into the desert, you should be able to avoid becoming lost.

The bad news:
You can survive for only three or four days without water. You need a lot of water to survive in the hot sun (4 gallons a day if the temperature is 100° F and you are working hard). Deserts are often very hot during the day and very cold at night. Many types of venomous snakes and insects live in deserts.

FIELD AGENT REPORT

How to avoid deadly desert peril:

☠ Be prepared: bring plenty of water and nonperishable food, a flashlight, a shovel, and a fully charged phone.

☠ If you are traveling in a vehicle, bring extra fuel.

☠ Make sure someone knows where you are going and when you're due back.

☠ If you break down in a vehicle, it's better to stay with it—rescuers will find a vehicle easier to spot.

☠ Conserve your energy.

☠ Protect yourself from the sun with a hat, loose-fitting clothing, and sunscreen.

☠ Learn some desert survival techniques— how to find water inside plants, for example.

☠ Use a mirror to signal to planes and spell out an SOS sign with rocks or other material.

Fact file:
Deserts are regions that receive very little rainfall, which doesn't necessarily mean they are hot places: the world's largest desert is the Antarctic, which is nearly one and a half times the size of the world's largest hot desert, the Sahara in Africa. Deserts cover about a third of the surface of the Earth.

UNEXPECTED PERILS

You probably wouldn't expect to be
struck on the head by a plummeting
reptile, killed by a coconut,
or to suddenly burst into flames.
But, as this section reveals,
you really never can tell.

Peril: Meteorite

Peril rating: 1/10

Location: Worldwide

Best known for: Careering through space to cause large-scale destruction on Earth

Your predicament:
You're out shopping one busy Saturday afternoon when you notice several people pointing up at the sky. You look up to see a large boulder hurtling toward you from above.

What's the worst that can happen?
A large lump of debris from the asteroid belt has made it through Earth's atmosphere and, although greatly reduced in size, it still weighs 220 pounds . . .

1. Unfortunately, it's heading for you.
2. You run to take shelter, but you're not fast enough.
3. You take a direct hit and are squashed flat.
4. You die.

The good news:
This is extremely unlikely to happen. There are no recorded incidents of anyone being killed by a meteorite. Most meteorites are very small, and you'd need a direct hit for even one of the bigger ones to kill you.

The bad news:
Meteorites are the least of your worries. Asteroids and comets, meteorites' heftier relations, can be so big that if one hit the Earth, no matter where, the dust created could block out sunlight and end life on the planet. An asteroid or comet large enough to cause mass extinction is expected to collide with the Earth about once every 100 million years, which means we're about due for one. (An asteroid was probably responsible for wiping out the dinosaurs.)

FIELD AGENT REPORT

How to avoid deadly meteorite peril:

☠ There is nothing you can do to avoid a direct hit from a meteorite, apart from remaining vigilant and perhaps wearing a hard hat.

There are several courses of action that can be taken to stop asteroids and comets from crashing into the Earth, however:

☠ Asteroids and comets on a collision course with Earth can be spotted with telescopes while they are still far enough away to give us time to prepare.

☠ Diverting a menacing asteroid from its course might be achieved by sending a spacecraft on a collision course, or using rockets or explosions to change its orbit.

☠ If an asteroid were to be found that was on course to collide with Earth in the next ten to a hundred years, we'd have an excellent chance of changing its course. However, if it were only a year away, there wouldn't be much we could do to stop it.

Fact file:

Meteorites consist of rock and metal. Most meteorites come from the asteroid belt between Jupiter and Mars, and a few from the Moon or Mars. They can weigh anything from a few grams to 220 pounds. Asteroids are also made of rock and metal but are much bigger—they might measure several miles across. Comets are like asteroids but are covered with ice and other compounds.

Peril: **Fugu**

Peril rating: 1/10

Location: Mainly Japan and South Korea

Best known for: Striking down diners with its fatal toxin

Your predicament:
You're visiting Japan for the first time and want to sample some of the country's famous dishes. You have heard that "fugu," or puffer fish, is a Japanese delicacy and want to try it for yourself.

What's the worst that can happen?
You are served torafugu, the most dangerous variety of fugu there is . . .

1. The waiter reminds you that the chef deliberately leaves a tiny amount of poison in the fish to create the unique and sought-after "tingle."
2. While eating the fish, you do feel a tingling on your lips and tongue.
3. Then you become dizzy and feel weak, with a headache and nausea.
4. Your body becomes completely paralyzed.
5. You are fully aware of everything around you but cannot move or speak.
6. You become unable to breathe. It seems that the chef left a little too much poison in the fish.
7. You die.

The good news:
Only highly trained chefs are allowed to prepare fugu. Not everyone poisoned by the fish dies—up to 50% of victims survive. Although there have been several deaths per year in the past (over 150 in 1958), the number has greatly decreased ever since the preparation of fugu has been regulated by the Japanese government.

The bad news:
Puffer fish contain deadly poison that paralyzes muscles: the victim remains fully conscious though unable to move, and eventually becomes unable to breathe. There is no antivenom. Most people poisoned by puffer fish are dead within 24 hours.

FIELD AGENT REPORT

How to avoid deadly fugu peril:

☠ To be completely sure of avoiding fugu poisoning, don't eat it.

☠ There won't be much you can do if you've been poisoned, but someone else should get you to a hospital as fast as possible.

☠ The only treatment available if you've been poisoned is to be put on life support until the poison wears off.

Fact file:
Fugu chefs need a special license to prepare fugu—they serve an apprenticeship for two to three years, then take a rigorous exam, which has a low pass rate. Torafugu has been eaten for thousands of years in Japan, though it was banned twice in Japanese history. The Japanese emperor is forbidden from eating it. The poison contained in fugu is tetrotodoxin (TTX), the same kind found in the blue-ringed octopus, which works on the nervous system.

Peril: Frozen Toilet Waste

Peril rating: 1/10

Location: Worldwide

Best known for: Hurtling toward Earth as especially unpleasant missiles

Your predicament:

You're in Frankfurt, Germany, walking down a busy main road.

What's the worst that can happen?

You are incredibly unlucky and are suddenly hit on the head by something very heavy and cold . . .

1. You have received a direct hit by frozen toilet waste from an international passenger aircraft.
2. You are vaguely aware of an unpleasant public-lavatory sort of smell before . . .
3. You sustain massive head injuries.
4. You die.

The good news:

Planes are not allowed to eject toilet waste. There are no records of anyone ever being directly hit by frozen toilet waste from a plane.

The bad news:

There have been various cases of homes and boats being hit by toilet waste from planes, possibly because the storage tank becomes overloaded and overflows to the outside of the aircraft, where it remains frozen to the fuselage until the plane descends as it approaches its destination, and the warmer air causes the ice to melt enough to fall off. How long until there's a direct hit to someone's head?

FIELD AGENT REPORT

How to avoid deadly toilet waste peril:

☠ You could reduce your chances of meeting this horrible fate by making sure you don't live near an airport.

☠ Otherwise, there's not much you can do, apart from wearing a crash helmet at all times, which would also keep you covered in case of a stray meteorite and various other falling-object hazards.

Fact file:
Aircraft use vacuum toilets that deposit waste in a holding tank. Once on the ground, the holding tank is emptied and the waste taken to a sewage works. It isn't possible for the aircraft crew to eject toilet waste while in flight, and the valve to the tank is usually on the outside of the plane. Toilet waste from aircraft is euphemistically known as "blue ice," because of the color of the toilet disinfectant.The busiest airport in the world is Hartsfield-Jackson Atlanta International Airport, in Georgia. It handles an average of 83.5 million passengers every year. Other very busy airports include London Heathrow, Los Angeles International, and Frankfurt International.

Peril: The Bermuda Triangle

Peril rating: 2/10

Location: The area of ocean contained in the triangle between Puerto Rico, Miami, and Bermuda

Best known for: Mysterious disappearances

Your predicament:
You are on board a ship sailing from Bermuda to an island in the Bahamas—right through the middle of the Bermuda Triangle.

What's the worst that can happen?
A tropical storm has been brewing for some time. Just as it arrives, the ship's navigational and other electrical equipment fails—no one knows why . . .

1. The storm is severe, sending huge waves crashing over the ship.
2. Badly damaged, the ship can't cope with the heavy seas and the captain gives the order to abandon ship.
3. As everyone rushes for the lifeboats, they are swept away by the storm.
4. The ship sinks, lost with all hands.
5. Everyone dies.

The good news:
Whatever the spooky rumors, statistically the Bermuda Triangle is no more dangerous than any other area of ocean, according to the marine insurance company Lloyds of London, who aren't known for taking chances. Some of the mysterious disappearances attributed to the Bermuda Triangle actually happened in other places entirely—for example, the "ghost ship" *Mary Celeste* is often associated with the Bermuda Triangle but in fact was found off the coast of Portugal.

The bad news:
This area is prone to tropical storms and hurricanes, and there are also strong currents produced by the Gulf Stream.

FIELD AGENT REPORT

How to avoid deadly Bermuda Triangle peril:

☠ Ensure that your craft is able to withstand severe storms, and that its navigational equipment is in good working order.

☠ If you are on board ship, make sure that it is well equipped for stormy weather.

☠ If you're really worried about it, you could just avoid the area—though this might send you on a rather long detour.

Fact file:

The Bermuda Triangle, about 440,000 square miles of ocean, was given its name in the 1960s. Perhaps the most famous early Triangle disappearance was the loss of "Flight 19," a 1945 military training exercise that ended with five planes lost. In common with other incidents in the area, the wreckage was never found, probably because the deepest part of the Atlantic Ocean lies close by. People have theorized that the Bermuda Triangle could be a hotspot for alien abduction. Others wonder if the lost City of Atlantis, a mythical civilization that was submerged by the sea, could be in some strange way responsible. The area's coast guards blame bad weather.

Peril: Tortoise-Dropping Birds

Peril rating: 1/10

Location: Europe, Asia, North Africa, the Middle East, North America

Best known for: Flattening an ancient Greek

Your predicament:
You're hiking in a remote, mountainous region of Turkey, where birds of prey swoop from the mountains to feed. You have already spotted golden eagles and bearded vultures.

What's the worst that can happen?
While you are hiking through the difficult terrain, a bearded vulture has picked up a tortoise, planning to drop it on the rocks below to break the creature's shell, then eat it . . .

1. In an unlucky turn of events, the bird drops the tortoise onto the very rock you are about to climb.
2. The tortoise lands directly on your head.
3. Dropped from a great height, the reptile fractures your skull.
4. You die.

The good news:
This is so unlikely to happen that you probably have more chance of winning the lottery while being eaten by a shark that's being attacked by a giant squid (exact figures unavailable). Legend has it that the ancient Greek dramatist Aeschylus was killed when an eagle dropped a tortoise on his head, but this is the only example that we know about.

The bad news:
There's no actual reason why you shouldn't fall prey to a falling tortoise if you are in bearded vulture or golden eagle habitat—bearded vultures have been known to pick up tortoises and drop them to break their shells, and there is evidence to suggest that golden eagles do the same. Bearded vultures are better known for dropping animal bones to get at the marrow, and a heavy bone dropped from a great height could also kill you. Bearded vultures also have a reputation for forcing people off cliffs—though this hasn't been proved.

FIELD AGENT REPORT

How to avoid deadly tortoise peril:

☠ If you find yourself in remote mountainous regions that are home to both tortoises and bearded vultures and/or golden eagles: be vigilant.

☠ Consider wearing a crash helmet.

☠ Try not to resemble a rock in any way.

Fact file:
The bearded vulture lives in mountainous regions of southern Europe, the Middle East, Africa, and Asia. It has a wingspan of up to about 10 feet. It lives on carrion and is especially fond of bone marrow, and even has a specially shaped tongue to extract it. Another name for the bearded vulture is "Bone Crusher" because of its habit of dropping bones from a great height. The golden eagle lives in mountains, deserts, and plateaus all over the northern hemisphere. It preys on small mammals and, occasionally, reptiles. Its wingspan is up to about 8 feet.

Peril: Spontaneous Human Combustion

Peril rating: 1/10

Location: Worldwide

Best known for: Incinerating random victims

Your predicament:
You're not feeling well so you've taken cold remedies that have made you drowsy. You settle down in front of the TV in an armchair, close to an open log fire.

What's the worst that can happen?
Unfortunately, you are about to become a rare statistic . . .

1. You lapse into unconsciousness.
2. Some time later, the police arrive to discover your charred remains: a pair of slippers is all that is left of you. The rest of the room is untouched by fire.
3. No one knows what really happened. But one thing is for certain: you are dead.

The good news:
It's by no means certain that Spontaneous Human Combustion (SHC) actually exists at all: instead of a mysterious phenomenon, suspected cases of SHC may simply be avoidable fires. Cases of suspected Spontaneous Human Combustion are very rare.

The bad news:
There have been suspected cases of SHC that are very difficult to otherwise explain—perhaps it really is possible to burst into flames for no reason. In that respect, we could all be at risk at any time.

FIELD AGENT REPORT

How to avoid deadly spontaneous combustion peril:

☠ Avoid sitting near fires in a drugged condition.

☠ Don't smoke (this is pretty good advice anyway): most suspected victims of SHC were smokers.

☠ Keep a bucket of water close at hand at all times.

☠ Make sure you have a working smoke alarm.

Fact file:

Skeptics argue that there is always a perfectly reasonable explanation for SHC. In many cases of suspected SHC, the human body is almost completely burned to ashes, meaning that the fire had to be extremely hot, while the surroundings show hardly any signs of fire damage. Experiments have shown that it is possible for a human body to burn like a candle, known as the "wick effect," due to the flammable material inside the body. Many cases of suspected SHC could be explained by the presence of nearby cigarettes or fires, a drugged or already-dead victim, and the wick effect. However, other cases seem to defy rational explanation.

Peril: Coconut

Peril rating: 2/10

Location: Tropical regions worldwide

Best known for: Hanging menacingly in coconut palms

Your predicament:
You're on vacation in the Caribbean. It is a warm, sunny day and you decide to have a nap in the shade.

What's the worst that can happen?
You soon fall asleep. Unfortunately, this means you don't hear the cracking sound from above you as a coconut gets ready to fall to the ground . . .

1. The coconut, weighing 5 pounds, drops from high up in the tree and strikes you directly on the head with great force.
2. You suffer a massive head injury.
3. You die.

The good news:
Despite various rumors about deadly coconut statistics, there does not seem to be any evidence of widespread deaths from falling coconuts. Before a coconut falls to the ground it usually makes a characteristic cracking sound that gives you warning to get out of the way. Your chances of being hit by a falling coconut and being killed as a result are extremely remote.

The bad news:
If you were underneath a coconut palm and received a direct hit to the head from a ripe coconut, the force would certainly be enough to kill you. Even if the falling coconut doesn't cause death to someone standing underneath the palm, it can inflict nasty injuries.

FIELD AGENT REPORT

How to avoid deadly coconut peril:

☠ Don't sleep underneath coconut palms.

☠ If you are especially worried about the perils of coconuts, avoid coconut palms altogether.

☠ You could take the extremely cautious approach of wearing protective headgear if you are in an area where there are coconut palms. Just in case.

Fact file:

Coconuts are the seeds of the coconut palm, which grows in tropical regions all over the world. They grow well in coastal areas because they are tolerant of sea salt and sandy soil. Coconuts are used for food (the flesh, coconut water, coconut oil, and coconut milk) and can also be used as fuel and to make ropes and mats. The Philippines is the world's largest coconut producer.

Peril: **Solar Flare**

Peril rating: 1/10

Location: Worldwide

Best known for: Emitting lethal radiation that could engulf the Earth

Your predicament:

You're on a long-haul flight not far from your final destination at a busy international airport, when suddenly the effects of a huge solar flare reach Earth.

What's the worst that can happen?

If you're extremely unlucky . . .

1. The plane's navigational equipment has just been rendered useless by the impact of radiation on the Earth's satellites caused by the solar flare.
2. Radio communication has also been affected.
3. Confused and unable to communicate with the control tower, the pilot is unaware of a second plane passing very close by.
4. The two planes collide.
5. You die.

The good news:

Luckily for us, solar flares happen all the time with no dangerous effects felt on Earth, because of the Earth's protective magnetic field and atmosphere. The chances of a solar flare big enough to dangerously affect life on our planet are extremely remote. The biggest solar flares recorded caused spectacular auroras (Northern and Southern lights) at the Earth's poles, not mass destruction.

The bad news:

Very big solar flares could injure any astronauts outside Earth's atmosphere. A really big solar flare could seriously affect navigational and radio equipment, causing potential peril for planes.

FIELD AGENT REPORT

How to avoid deadly solar flare peril:

☠ Other than moving to Uranus, there's not very much you, or anybody else, can do to avoid explosions on the surface of the sun.

☠ But there is a time difference between the observation of a solar flare and its potentially disruptive effects on Earth: hopefully, this will give you enough warning to ensure you're not on a plane.

☠ Or it could give the pilot the chance to avoid busy flight paths at the time when navigation and radio equipment is likely to be affected.

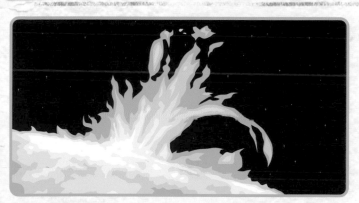

Fact file:
A solar flare is an explosion in the sun's atmosphere (explosions also happen in the atmospheres of other stars), when material is heated to many millions of degrees and as much energy is released as 10 billion hydrogen bombs. The flares occur near sunspots (areas of intense magnetic activity on the sun's surface), and can emit radiation that affects the upper part of the Earth's atmosphere, as well as satellites outside the atmosphere. Frequency and strength of solar flares vary according to an 11-year cycle. The Earth's atmosphere and magnetic field protects it from solar flares.

ANIMAL ATTACKS

Whether you're canoeing in Botswana
or trekking in North America,
ferocious beasts lie menacingly
in wait, ready to chew off
your arm (or your head).

Peril: Fierce Snake

Peril rating: 4/10

Location: Central Australia

Best known for: Being the world's most venomous snake

Your predicament:

You're in a cane plantation in the west of Queensland, Australia. Unwittingly, you have stepped on the tail of a long brown snake, which strikes repeatedly at your ankle.

What's the worst that can happen?

You have been bitten by an Inland Taipan, or Fierce Snake, which has the most toxic venom of any snake in the world . . .

1. You try to apply a pressure bandage but, as no one is there to help you, the movement makes you feel worse.
2. As the poison spreads through your body you experience headache, stomachache, nausea, and vomiting.
3. You feel dizzy and your vision is blurred.
4. You start to have convulsions.
5. You lapse into a coma and die.

The good news:

The Inland Taipan lives in remote regions of Australia, so it seldom comes into contact with people. It is not aggressive, though it will strike if cornered or threatened. This snake has shorter fangs than some other species, so not as much poison is delivered. Antivenom exists, so if you get to the hospital quickly you will be safe. Despite the strength of the Fierce Snake's venom, there has never been a recorded human death from its bite.

The bad news:

Although it isn't the most deadly snake in the world (the carpet viper probably kills the most people), it is the most venomous: the venom delivered in a single bite from an Inland Taipan is enough to kill 100 people—50 times stronger than an Indian cobra's bite. Fierce Snakes are large and move fast. The poison works quickly and, among other things, destroys muscle tissue, which can lead to kidney failure. Even if you survive a bite, you may be left with permanent organ damage.

How to avoid deadly snake peril:

☠ If you see any type of snake, you should keep away from it, especially in Australia, which is home to the world's top ten most venomous snakes.

If you are bitten:

☠ Don't wash the wound. When you get to the hospital, a swab will be taken to identify the type of snake.

☠ Keep the bite lower than the heart if possible.

☠ Never apply a tourniquet, cut the wound, or try to suck out the poison.

☠ Move as little as possible to avoid spreading the venom.

☠ If the bite is on a limb apply a broad bandage with a firm pressure. Use a splint or sling so that the limb moves as little as possible.

☠ Get to the hospital immediately.

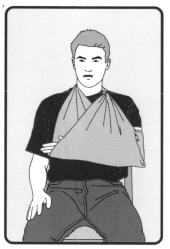

Fact file:
The Inland Taipan lives in the hot, dry grasslands and plains. A fully grown Fierce Snake can be up to 8 feet long. The snakes do not have colorful patterns: they are usually dark brown or olive green. They feed on rodents.

Peril: Crocodile

Peril rating: 8/10

Location: Rivers and estuaries of tropical and southern Africa and Madagascar

Best known for: Lurking in rivers, barely visible, before launching a vicious attack on anyone or anything close to the water

Your predicament:
You are in Egypt. It's a beautiful evening and, just as the sun is setting, you decide to go down to the banks of the River Nile to watch the Egyptian boats, feluccas, drift by.

What's the worst that can happen?
As you stand on the riverbank taking in the scenery, you notice a small movement in the water close by. The next second, you are grabbed by a large and ferocious crocodile . . .

1. The crocodile lunges at your shoulder, takes hold, and drags you into the river.
2. You are pulled underwater and shaken vigorously.
3. You drown.
4. The crocodile eats you.

The good news:
Many species of crocodile are not dangerous unless provoked. A crocodile can't easily open its mouth if you succeed in clamping it shut.

The bad news:
Crocodiles have a stronger bite than any other animal—including great white sharks. They are surprisingly fast on land, in short bursts, and extremely fast in water. They also have sharp claws. Crocodiles are one of the few species to see humans as prey. The animals can be difficult to spot as they lurk with only their eyes and nostrils above water. They can cooperate with one another to kill prey. Crocodiles often live close to people and as a result there are many human deaths per year.

FIELD AGENT REPORT

How to avoid deadly crocodile peril:

☠ Don't enter ponds, water holes, streams, rivers, estuaries, or lakes if you are in an area known for crocodiles, especially at night.

☠ Never go anywhere near baby crocodiles.

☠ If a crocodile gets close to you, run away in a straight line.

☠ If there's a tree nearby, climb it.

☠ You won't be able to outswim a crocodile—stay out of the water.

☠ If you are able to, hold the crocodile's mouth closed and hope that help arrives before other crocodiles do.

☠ If a crocodile attacks you, try bashing its nose, poking it in the eyes, and screaming.

Fact file:

Nile crocodiles can reach 20 feet long and weigh around 1,100 pounds. They eat mostly fish, but will attack large mammals and birds and also eat carrion. They can eat half their body weight in one meal. They can run at about 9 mph (though not for very long) and swim at 22 mph. In the wild, they live for about 45 years. Saltwater crocodiles, which live in eastern India, Bangladesh, Southeast Asia, Papua New Guinea, and Australia, are even bigger. The largest one on record was 28 feet long.

Peril: Hippopotamus

Peril rating: 8/10

Location: African rivers, lakes, and wetlands south of North Africa

Best known for: Snapping boats in half with its gigantic jaws

Your predicament:

You're canoeing in the swamps of Botswana. You hear a grunting sound and, as you round a bend in the reeds, you find yourself face-to-face with a huge, angry-looking hippo.

What's the worst that can happen?

You have annoyed one of Africa's most dangerous animals . . .

1. The hippo opens its jaws, exposing enormous teeth. It bellows and swings its huge head from side to side.
2. The animal advances toward you menacingly and with surprising speed.
3. You try to paddle away in your canoe, but you're not fast enough.
4. The hippo lunges at the canoe and takes an enormous bite.
5. You die instantly.

The good news:

Hippos are vegetarian, so at least they won't see you as a tasty snack. Not all encounters with hippos have ended in instant death: sometimes the hippo remains peacefully where it is, or the hippo might open its jaws as a warning before retreating, or it might maim but not kill its victim. Hippos often back off after biting, at least allowing the person to escape (assuming he or she can move).

The bad news:

Hippos are very territorial and aggressive, and they don't like humans trespassing on their patch. They are extremely large and powerful, with enormous sharp teeth that have been known to bite a crocodile in half. If they think you are a threat, they are likely to bite first, think later. They are fast and agile in water. Even on land, you won't outrun a hippo.

FIELD AGENT REPORT

How to avoid deadly hippo peril:

☠ Stay away from hippo habitats.

☠ If you do see hippos, keep as far away as possible and don't make any loud noises or threatening movements.

☠ Hippos open their jaws as a warning: they are not yawning. If you see a hippo open its jaws, retreat as quickly as you can.

☠ Hippos are most dangerous when they feel cut off from water or their young. Make sure you're not blocking the animal's route.

Fact file:
There are two species of hippo, the common and the pygmy hippo, but only the common kind is dangerous to humans. Hippos are in competition with the white rhino to be the second largest land mammal after the elephant. Male hippos can weigh up to 3.5 tons, and measure up to 5 feet tall and 11 feet long. Their cavernous mouths can open more than 3 feet wide, revealing teeth up to 28 inches long. At a sprint over short distances, hippos can run on land at up to 17 mph.

Peril: Elephant

Peril rating: 7/10

Location: Sub-Saharan East and Central Africa

Best known for: Terrifying charges and spearing victims with huge tusks

Your predicament:

You're on safari in Tanzania at the Serengeti National Park. Suddenly you spot what you've been looking for—a magnificent herd of elephants.

What's the worst that can happen?

You leave the safari jeep to get a better photograph, still a safe distance away. Suddenly . . .

1. A lone male elephant emerges from the bush. It trumpets and rushes toward you.
2. You are gored repeatedly by the elephant's long, powerful tusks.
3. The elephant ends the attack by kneeling on your body.
4. You die.

The good news:

If you are careful not to provoke an attack, you probably won't be the victim of a charging elephant. Elephants are vegetarian and won't see you as food. They often "mock charge"—they are more likely to do this if their ears are sticking out. People do survive being charged by an elephant.

The bad news:

Elephants are the largest land animal on Earth: the biggest ever recorded measured 13 feet at the shoulder and weighed 11 tons. They can be aggressive, and once a year male elephants go into "musth," the mating season, when they become especially aggressive. Elephants can run at 25 mph, so you won't be able to escape. Elephants' natural habitat is constantly diminishing, which leads to more attacks on people. Both African and Indian elephants kill hundreds of people every year.

FIELD AGENT REPORT

How to avoid deadly elephant peril:

☠ Stay in your vehicle.

☠ If you are being threatened, hide behind nearby rocks or termite mounds—if the elephant can't see you it will feel less threatened. If you are on foot and see an elephant, try to stay downwind.

☠ Move slowly away.

☠ Don't run—the elephant can run faster than you.

☠ Climb a big tree— you'll need to climb quite high to be out of the elephant's reach, though, and the tree will need to be big enough that the elephant can't knock it over.

Fact file:

Male African savannah elephants measure about 11 feet at the shoulder and weigh 6.5 tons on average. Asian elephants are smaller, and there is also a slightly smaller African species, the forest elephant. Adult male elephants tend to live alone, while female elephants and their calves live in groups. The animals have complicated social interactions and use a variety of sounds and gestures to communicate. They live up to about 70 years in the wild, feeding on grass, roots, and bark—up to 285 pounds in just one day.

Peril: Grizzly Bear

Peril rating: 6/10

Location: North America

Best known for: Standing on hind legs, snarling, and looking terrifyingly huge

Your predicament:
You are hiking in the Alaskan wilderness—bear country . . .

What's the worst that can happen?
By accident, you surprise a female grizzly bear with her cub . . .

1. The bear stands on its hind legs, sniffing and looking menacing.
2. You back away slowly, then fear gets the better of you and you run as fast as you can.
3. The bear runs after you and easily catches up with you.
4. You are mauled to death.

The good news:
Grizzly bears usually avoid people, and don't prey on them as food (even though they're more than capable of killing and eating humans). They won't attack unless surprised, or if a mother is protecting her cubs, which is the most common reason for attack. The bear wants to remove you as a threat, not eat you (at least, not usually).

The bad news:
Grizzly bears are considered to be the most aggressive bears of all. They are huge, ferocious when provoked, and can easily kill an animal your size. They can outrun you. Grizzly bears do attack humans sometimes in order to eat them. Because they need to store enough fat for their hibernation, bears are always on the lookout for food— even if this doesn't include you, it will include whatever's in your backpack.

FIELD AGENT REPORT

How to avoid deadly grizzly bear peril:

☠ As you hike, make lots of noise.

☠ Don't leave food lying around: hang it high up in a tree, or use a bear-proof storage container.

☠ If you see a bear, keep as far away from it as you can, especially if it has cubs.

If you are confronted with an angry grizzly:

☠ Climb a tree—most grizzlies can't.

☠ Back away slowly, talking to the bear—but don't make eye contact, which could be seen as a sign of aggression.

☠ Don't run away, as the bear is likely to run after you—and they can run faster.

☠ If you are forced to run from a grizzly, run downhill—the bear's mass of muscle behind its forelegs makes it more difficult for it to run downhill.

☠ Bear spray, a bit like pepper spray, can be effective.

☠ If the grizzly attacks, play dead. But if it continues to maul, your only option is to fight back.

Fact file:

The grizzly bear gets its name from the gray ("grizzled") tips to its fur. Male grizzlies can reach 8 feet tall standing up, and weigh up to about 790 pounds. In the wild they live to about 25 years. They are fast runners—up to 30 mph. They tend to be solitary, apart from female bears with cubs. Like all brown bears, they hibernate in winter. Most of the grizzly's diet consists of plants, but they also eat animals as big as moose.

Peril: **Lion**

Peril rating: 7/10

Location: Plains throughout Sub-Saharan Africa

Best known for: Stealthy, bloody, and usually deadly ambush attacks

Your predicament:
You're on vacation in South Africa, sightseeing in Kruger National Park, when you spot a pride of lions. You can't resist leaving the jeep for a photo opportunity—the lions look sleepy and bored and, you reason, they probably see so many tourists that they're used to them.

What's the worst that can happen?
You count the lions, and wonder if there weren't a couple more than that a minute ago . . .

1. Some well-camouflaged lionesses have moved into position behind long grass.
2. They attack with astonishing speed.
3. You are brought down, mauled, and a quick bite to your neck crushes your windpipe.
4. You die.

The good news:
Lions do not usually attack humans. It is possible to survive a lion attack, though without a spear or other weapon you will be very lucky to do so. Lions do most of their hunting at night, so during the day you should be relatively safe.

The bad news:
Lionesses are skillful predators and hunt in a group. Occasionally a male lion will seek out humans to eat (possibly due to illness, or depletion of natural habitat or prey). Lions kill hundreds of people every year in African countries. If you are attacked by a lion, the likelihood is that it will kill you.

How to avoid deadly lion peril:

☠ Stay inside your safari vehicle.

☠ If camping, never leave your tent at night and avoid turning on your flashlight.

☠ Look out for fresh lion droppings or footprints.

☠ Follow safety advice given to you by your guide— this will almost certainly include keeping away from carnivorous wild animals.

Fact file:
Lions are found only in African national parks and game reserves. There are also Asiatic lions, an endangered species found only in the Gir Forest in the state of Gujarat in northern India. Big male lions can be up to 7 feet long, 4 feet tall at the shoulder, and weigh around 550 pounds. Lions are the only big cats to live in groups (called prides). They work as a group to ambush their prey, which might be antelope, zebra, or warthogs, and sometimes they also scavenge for food. In the wild, lions live for about 15 years.

Peril: Golden Poison Frog

Peril rating: 4/10

Location: Colombian rainforest

Best known for: Being the most poisonous creature on the planet

Your predicament:
You are trekking through the humid rainforests of Colombia when you see a bright yellow frog, just a couple of inches long, sitting on a log. You reach out your hand to touch it.

What's the worst that can happen?
The frog is an extremely toxic golden poison frog . . .

1. The poison on the frog's skin irritates your skin—you begin to scratch, breaking your skin slightly.
2. The poison is quickly absorbed into your bloodstream.
3. Your muscles begin to contract.
4. Your heart fails.
5. You die.

The good news:
You need to touch the frog to be poisoned—the frog won't leap out at you and rub itself on your skin. And even then, the poison has to get into your bloodstream—it's possible to handle a golden poison frog without being poisoned (though it's not recommended). There aren't many of these animals around, which you might think is good news for you, but it is very bad news for the frog, which is an endangered species.

The bad news:
The golden poison frog is the most poisonous animal in the world: each frog contains enough poison to kill ten adult humans. If you have even a tiny cut or abrasion on your skin, or if you accidentally touch your mouth after touching the frog, the poison will enter your bloodstream and kill you, probably in a matter of minutes. There is no antivenom.

FIELD AGENT REPORT

How to avoid deadly frog peril:

☠ Don't touch ANY brightly colored frog. Although the golden poison frog is the most toxic, many other types of poisonous frogs exist in the rainforests of South America.

☠ Always cover any wounds, however minor, when you are hiking in the jungle.

☠ If you have been poisoned, your only hope is to get to the hospital as soon as you can.

Fact file:

The golden poison frog is found only in the rainforests in Colombia. The frogs can be bright yellow, orange, or, despite the name, green or white. They reach 2 inches in length and contain about a milligram of poison in their skin glands, but that's enough to kill several adults. Anything that eats the frog will die, though there is one type of snake that has developed some immunity to the poison. Local people use the poison to put on their arrows. In captivity, the frogs lose their toxicity—there could be a tiny creature central to the golden poison frog's diet that gives it its poison, and perhaps it's this creature that's actually the most poisonous animal on Earth.

Peril: Cape Buffalo

Peril rating: 8/10

Location: Sub-Saharan Africa north of South Africa

Best known for: Looking like a big, gentle cow but in fact being one of the most dangerous animals in Africa

Your predicament:
You're on vacation in Kenya. It's dusk and, from your hotel balcony, you spot a herd of large, docile-looking cows in the grounds. You decide to take a stroll.

What's the worst that can happen?
You go outside, ignoring an agitated hotel employee who seems to be trying to tell you something . . .

1. You walk a short way from the hotel and soon realize that the cows are in fact buffalo.
2. One of them turns to face you, snorts, and begins to charge.
3. You run away as fast as you can, but the animal easily outruns you.
4. The Cape buffalo gores you with its sharp horns, and finally stamps on you.
5. You die.

The good news:
If you aren't reckless enough to get close to Cape buffalo without the protection of a vehicle or a sturdy building, you won't be harmed.

The bad news:
Despite being vegetarian, Cape buffalo are extremely dangerous. They are fiercely territorial and aggressive and, once they begin an attack, very persistent. The animals are fast and powerful, with sharp, deadly horns. They can defend themselves against lions—and sometimes kill them.

FIELD AGENT REPORT

How to avoid deadly buffalo peril:

☠ Stay away from Cape buffalo territory unless you are with a guided tour.

☠ If you do see Cape buffalo, keep your distance and never approach them.

☠ Running away won't do you any good—climb a tree. Take extra care during the hottest part of the day— this is when buffalo like to rest, and if they are surprised by people they will be even more angry than usual.

Fact file:
Cape buffalo are the largest of the antelope family. They can measure up to about 12 feet long and 6 feet tall, and the biggest males can weigh up to a ton. They live mostly on grass and often feed at night, resting during the heat of the day. Female Cape buffalo and their young live in herds of up to a thousand strong, while adult males tend to live on their own. They are fiercely protective of their calves and one another.

Peril: Vampire Bat

Peril rating: 3/10

Location: Central and South America

Best known for: Nocturnal blood-sucking

Your predicament:

On vacation in the Argentinian countryside, you wake up one morning and notice a small, neat cut on your leg. You know this is an area inhabited by vampire bats, which live exclusively on the blood of large mammals.

What's the worst that can happen?

You have been bitten by a disease-carrying vampire bat . . .

1. Three weeks after being bitten, you feel a tingling pain around the cut.
2. During the next few days you start to feel anxious and sensitive to light and loud noises.
3. Within another week, you find it increasingly difficult to swallow and become afraid of water. You become more and more paranoid and start to hallucinate.
4. You find it very difficult to swallow saliva, and have periods of thrashing about, biting, and spitting.
5. These are symptoms of the disease rabies. Soon you are completely paralyzed, fall into a coma, and die.

The good news:

Some vampire bats do carry rabies, but they usually feed on animals—commonly cows, donkeys, horses, sheep, and pigs—and only rarely bite humans. Two species of vampire bat feed mostly on birds. There is an effective rabies vaccine. If you are not vaccinated and are bitten by a rabies-carrying bat, there is also an effective treatment if it is given before symptoms start.

The bad news:

If you are bitten by a bat infected with the rabies virus and you are not vaccinated, the chances of survival are small unless you receive treatment before the onset of symptoms. You may not know you've been bitten—vampire bats usually manage to drink blood without waking the animal or person, and the cut they make in the skin is only about an eighth of an inch long. If treatment is not given before symptoms appear—usually between two and twelve weeks after being bitten—then the chances of survival are almost nil.

FIELD AGENT REPORT

How to avoid deadly vampire bat peril:

☠ If you are traveling to an area where there are known to be cases of rabies, make sure you get vaccinated against the disease.

☠ If you are sleeping outside, or inside with the windows open, use mosquito netting around your bed.

☠ If you think you have been bitten by a bat, see a doctor.

Fact file:

There are three species of bat that feed on blood: the common vampire bat and two others that feed mostly on the blood of birds. All three species live in Central and South America. Their bodies are only a couple of inches long and weigh up to 2 ounces. They feed by making a cut in the skin with their teeth, then lapping up the blood. Their saliva contains an anticoagulant that has been used in human medicine to help patients who have had strokes.

Peril: Cassowary Bird

Peril rating: 3/10

Location: Northeastern Australia, New Guinea

Best known for: Disemboweling jungle visitors

Your predicament:

You're trekking through the rainforest of northern Queensland, Australia. You hear rustling in the undergrowth and go to investigate. You spot a large, strange-looking bird with a bright blue and red crested head.

What's the worst that can happen?

You have encountered a cassowary bird . . .

1. You go closer, not realizing that the bird might be dangerous.
2. The bird feels threatened.
3. You continue to approach.
4. The bird suddenly runs at you at great speed, its legs outstretched in front of it.
5. The bird's claws inflict a horrible wound in your stomach.
6. You die.

The good news:

Cassowaries are generally shy birds, and as long as you don't threaten them, you will probably be safe. Cassowaries are quite rare—though of course this is bad news for the bird.

The bad news:

The cassowary is considered the world's most dangerous bird. It can be aggressive and will attack if it feels threatened, particularly if it is cornered. The cassowary has three big claws on each foot: the middle claw is 5 inches long, very sharp, and capable of disemboweling a large mammal. Cassowaries can run very fast.

FIELD AGENT REPORT

How to avoid deadly cassowary peril:

☠ If you are lucky enough to spot a cassowary, keep your distance.

☠ If you accidentally get close, back away slowly.

☠ If you think the cassowary is about to attack, it may help to raise your hands above your head to make yourself look taller.

☠ Keep something in front of you—for example, a tree branch—to stop the cassowary from reaching your body with its legs.

☠ Climb a tree—but remember that cassowaries can jump, even though they can't fly.

Fact file:

Cassowaries are flightless birds similar to emus. They eat plants, seeds, nuts, insects, and sometimes small animals. The female birds are bigger and more brightly colored—they can reach 7 feet tall and weigh up to about 155 pounds (the largest on record weighed 183 pounds). The male birds look after the eggs and young birds. Cassowaries can run at speeds of 30 mph, and they can jump 5 feet high. They live for up to 60 years in the wild.

Peril: Komodo Dragon

Peril rating: 2/10

Location: Indonesia

Best known for: Being terrifying oversized lizards with the worst breath in the animal kingdom

Your predicament:

You're on an island in southeastern Indonesia. You are walking along a trail when suddenly a huge, ugly lizard emerges from the bushes and lunges for your right leg.

What's the worst that can happen?

You have been attacked by a Komodo dragon . . .

1. You manage to pry open the creature's jaws and escape, with a horrible wound in your lower leg.
2. You get as far away from the reptile as you can but are forced to rest.
3. The wound in your leg becomes swollen and very painful.
4. You feel dizzy, cold, and clammy and develop diarrhea.
5. You die within a day or so. The Komodo dragon finds your body and eats it.

The good news:

More often than not the victim escapes, so unless you are on your own you will probably survive, as long as you receive medical attention quickly. If you are in good shape, you should be able to outrun a Komodo dragon. Attacks on humans are very rare—there have only ever been eight recorded attacks in the wild, and one recorded death in the last 35 years. There aren't many of the creatures left—only 3,000–5,000 in the wild (though this is not good news for the dragons).

The bad news:

The Komodo dragon injects a mild venom in its bite, which causes swelling and pain. But much more dangerous is the creature's saliva, which contains 50 different strains of virulent bacteria. An animal that's been bitten by a Komodo dragon usually dies within a few days from blood poisoning. The dragon follows the prey until it dies. Komodo dragons can run fast for short distances—up to about 13 mph—but they usually lurk by game trails, well camouflaged, to bring down their prey. If the dragon manages to bite your body or neck with its sharp serrated teeth, you may die right away.

How to avoid deadly dragon peril:

☠ Don't go into Komodo dragon territory on your own. Be on the alert for their presence.

☠ If you are attacked, you need to get medical attention as quickly as possible. The wound needs to be thoroughly cleaned and you need a hefty course of antibiotics immediately—the dragon's saliva is lethal.

Fact file:

Komodo dragons, members of the monitor lizard family, live only on four islands in southeastern Indonesia, on hot, dry grasslands. They are usually between 7 to 10 feet long and weigh 155 pounds, though they can weigh much more after a heavy meal—Komodo dragons can eat up to 80% of their own body weight in one meal. They have 60 1-inch-long serrated teeth, which are frequently replaced, like a shark's. They eat mostly carrion but also attack prey. Komodo dragons live for up to 50 years.

SMALL BUT LETHAL

They say good things come in
small packages, but so do creepy
crawly things that can inject
you with deadly poison before
you even know they're there.
And they outnumber all other
animals—there are millions
of insects for every human
being on the planet. What
are they planning?

Peril: Black Widow Spider

Peril rating: 3/10

Location: North America and Sweden

Best known for: Hiding in toilets, waiting to inflict a lethal bite

Your predicament:
You are in the bathroom of your home. As you lift up the toilet seat you feel a painful bite and see a small black spider with a red marking disappearing behind the water tank.

What's the worst that can happen?
You have been bitten by a black widow spider. During the next few hours . . .

1. You feel severe pain near the bite.
2. You start to ache all over.
3. You feel dizzy.
4. Your kidneys fail.
5. You lapse into a coma.
6. You die.

The good news:
Unless you are very young, very old, or sick, you are unlikely to die as a result of a bite from a black widow spider. Usually, symptoms will just go away a day or two after the bite without any treatment. Although their venom is powerful, black widow spiders are small and can't inject very much poison into your body through their tiny fangs. There is an antivenom. The spiders are not aggressive toward people.

The bad news:
Black widows are small and you might not notice them, or assume they are not dangerous. The venom is very painful. There is some debate about whether the antivenom may be more dangerous than the original spider bite—allergic reactions have led to deaths. Although complications are rare, bite victims can get worse and die very quickly. Black widow spiders are common and often lie in wait in dark places where you might touch them accidentally—on the undersides of rocks, garbage can lids, and toilet seats.

FIELD AGENT REPORT

How to avoid deadly spider peril:

☠ Be vigilant around black widow habitats: low-lying tree branches, piles of wood, basements, rarely used shoes.

☠ Learn to identify the web: an irregular, mesh web with a funnel-shaped opening at one end.

☠ Always go to the hospital if you think you have been bitten by a venomous spider.

Fact file:

There are three species of black widow, all of which are venomous. The spiders are small—less than 2 inches long. They live on insects and small reptiles and mammals. Male black widows are only half the size of females, and are sometimes eaten by them (hence the name). Black widows are found in the U.S. and Canada in urban environments as well as woodlands, and have recently become established in Sweden, possibly from cars imported from the U.S.

Peril: Killer Bees

Peril rating: 2/10

Location: South America and southern United States

Best known for: Attacking unfortunate passersby in deadly swarms

Your predicament:

You're taking a country walk in California and notice a low humming sound. A bee lands on your face—you swat it away but it has already stung you. Another bee lands on your ankle . . . and another . . . and another . . . Suddenly the air is thick with angry bees. Panicked, you jump into a nearby lake.

What's the worst that can happen?

The bees are Africanized honey bees (known as "killer bees") and . . .

1. Your position under the water won't help you—as soon as you come up for air, the bees are waiting.
2. You are stung repeatedly.
3. Although you aren't allergic to bee stings, the many hundreds of stings you receive cause an allergic reaction.
4. You die.

The good news:

The sting of an Africanized honey bee is no more toxic than an ordinary bee's. They can't fly very fast—you will be able to outrun them if you are in reasonably good shape. They might sound scary, but they have caused very few deaths. As long as you are fit and well, and not allergic to bee stings, you're very unlikely to die as a result of an encounter with so-called killer bees.

The bad news:

Africanized honey bees look just like ordinary honey bees but are much more aggressive. They will attack, often in very large numbers, if they think there's a threat within 90 feet or so of their hive. And they're pretty sensitive: they will feel threatened by loud noises, strong smells, shiny jewelry . . . or even just people nearby. When one bee stings, a chemical is released that causes other bees to sting. The bees chase you for up to a quarter of a mile. Some people are allergic to bee stings: if you are one of them, then any single bee sting, not necessarily from a killer bee, could kill you. For this reason, ordinary honey bees are one of the world's most dangerous insects.

FIELD AGENT REPORT

How to avoid deadly bee peril:

☠ Run away! Most healthy people can outrun Africanized bees.

☠ Protect your face—the bees tend to attack the face and ankles first.

☠ Don't jump in a lake or river to escape from the bees—they will still be there waiting for you when you come up for air.

☠ If your face begins to swell and breathing becomes difficult, seek immediate treatment for anaphylactic shock.

Fact file:
African bees were introduced to Brazil in the 1950s to breed a more productive type of honey bee. Some escaped and bred with native bees: the hybrids became known as Africanized honey bees. The bees have since spread from South America to the southern United States.

Peril: Anopheles Mosquito

Peril rating: 9/10

Location: Sub-Saharan Africa, South America, the Middle East, and parts of Europe

Best known for: The tiny, almost painless bite that spreads the biggest killer disease on the planet

Your predicament:

You're on vacation in the Gambia, West Africa, playing a game outside as dusk falls. You are bitten by numerous mosquitoes.

What's the worst that can happen?

One of the mosquitoes that bites you is an anopheles, and it is carrying malaria . . .

1. Ten days after the bite, when you're back home, you get a headache, fever, and flu symptoms.
2. You think you have the flu and don't bother going to see a doctor.
3. When you finally do go to see a doctor, you are diagnosed with the flu.
4. You experience sickness and diarrhea as well as flu-like symptoms.
5. You die.

The good news:

As long as you are diagnosed with malaria early enough and take medicine, malaria probably won't kill you. Malaria is caused by a parasite, which gets into the bloodstream via a mosquito's bite: there are four types, but only one of them causes malignant malaria. Benign malaria is less serious.

The bad news:

If you come from a malaria-free country, you are unlikely to have built up any immunity to the disease and you are especially at risk. Symptoms usually appear between ten days and four weeks after the bite, but can take up to a year to appear. In some parts of the world, the parasites that cause malaria have developed a resistance to some malaria medicines. Mosquitoes carry other potentially fatal diseases.

FIELD AGENT REPORT

How to avoid deadly mosquito peril:

If you are going to a country where malaria exists:

☠ Use a mosquito net over your bed at night.

☠ Spray insect repellent on exposed skin.

☠ Take anti-malaria tablets.

☠ Mosquitoes are most likely to be found around stagnant water, where they breed. Take care not to provide stagnant water for them, and keep away from ponds if you can.

Fact file:
Mosquitoes have existed for millions of years, during which time they've become very good at finding mammals, whose blood they suck through a long, thin tube. They can sense the presence of a mammal up to 120 feet away. Only the anopheles mosquito carries malaria. Mosquitoes are responsible for millions of deaths: over a million people die from malaria every year, mostly in Africa, because they aren't treated in time.

Peril: **Death Stalker Scorpion**

Peril rating: 3/10

Location: Northern Africa and the Middle East

Best known for: Lurking in dark places with a deadly sting in its tail

Your predicament:
You're on vacation seeing the sights of Jordan in the Middle East. As you get out of bed one morning, you put on your slippers and feel a painful sting in your toe. You withdraw your foot and a small yellow scorpion scuttles off.

What's the worst that can happen?
You have been stung by an extremely venomous scorpion, the death stalker . . .

1. Two hours after being stung, you feel your throat begin to swell.
2. You go back to bed, experiencing numbness and a rapid heart rate.
3. You have trouble breathing.
4. You begin to cough up blood.
5. You die.

The good news:
Unless you're very young, very old, or sick, you are unlikely to die after being stung by a death stalker. There is an antivenom. Only 3% of cases have a severe reaction to the sting. Most species of scorpion are not dangerous to humans.

The bad news:
The death stalker scorpion is one of the most venomous scorpions in the world. Some people have an allergic reaction to its poison, which can be fatal. The creature can be aggressive. A sting is extremely painful.

FIELD AGENT REPORT

How to avoid deadly scorpion peril:

☠ If you are in a country where scorpions live, always be careful where you step.

☠ Scorpions like to hide in dark places, so always check footwear before you put it on.

☠ Check your bed for scorpions before you get in. Sleep under a mosquito net to stop scorpions and other insects from biting you as you sleep.

☠ If you have been stung, get to the hospital as quickly as you can—antivenom may be needed.

Fact file:

The death stalker scorpion is yellow and up to about 4 inches long. The creatures feed on spiders and insects. The death stalker's small, weak pincers are the reason for its powerful venom: it needs the venom to paralyze the creatures it preys on, because its pincers aren't strong enough to do so. The size of any scorpion's pincers is a good way to measure the probable potency of its poison. The neurotoxins in death stalker scorpion venom are being studied in the hope of finding a treatment for brain cancer and diabetes.

Peril: Giant Centipede

Peril rating: 2/10

Location: Northern and western South America, Trinidad, and Jamaica

Best known for: Looking fearsome and way too big

Your predicament:

You're hiking in the Amazon rainforest, home to many thousands of different species of creepy-crawlies. You feel a tickling sensation on your leg and look down to see an enormous centipede disappearing up the leg of your shorts.

What's the worst that can happen?

As you desperately try to remove the horrible-looking creature, it bites you on the thigh . . .

1. You manage to remove the creature and continue on your way with a shudder.
2. The bite quickly becomes swollen and itchy.
3. You begin to feel hot and weak. Unfortunately, you are allergic to the venom and go into anaphylactic shock . . .
4. You develop an itchy rash all over your body.
5. Your face swells, and you feel a tightness in your throat and chest.
6. You lose consciousness.
7. You die.

The good news:

You are very unlikely to die as a result of a centipede bite, even if it's a giant centipede, unless you are very young, old, or sick.

The bad news:

A bite from any large centipede is extremely painful. Some people are allergic to centipede bites, which would cause the symptoms described above. If you are allergic to the venom, you can die unless you receive medical attention quickly. The centipedes move very fast.

FIELD AGENT REPORT

How to avoid deadly centipede peril:

☠ Make sure you are properly dressed for a hike in the rainforest: this will include covering your skin completely to protect it from biting insects, among other things.

☠ Apply plenty of insect repellent.

☠ Sleep under a mosquito net.

☠ If you are allergic to the venom, you need medical treatment immediately, which will involve an injection of adrenaline.

Fact file:
The Amazonian giant centipede can be a foot long, with between 42 and 46 yellow legs and a segmented, maroon-colored body. It eats insects, snails, and small animals such as lizards, frogs, and mice, and dangles from cave roofs to capture passing bats.

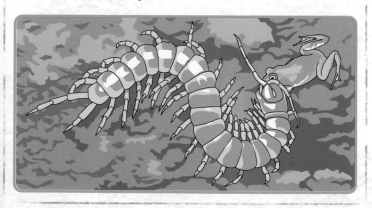

Peril: Tsetse Fly
Peril rating: 5/10
Location: Africa
Best known for: Spreading the dreaded sleeping sickness disease

Your predicament:
You are living in a remote part of Tanzania. Not for the first time, you feel a painful insect bite and assume it must have been a horsefly.

What's the worst that can happen?
You have been bitten by a tsetse fly. Unfortunately, the insect is infected with a parasite that causes the acute form of the disease sleeping sickness . . .

1. A few days after being bitten, you develop fever, headache, and joint pain.
2. You develop alarming swellings, most noticeably underneath your jawline and in your armpits (these are your lymph nodes).
3. Untreated, you develop anemia and heart and kidney problems.
4. Within a few months, you die.

The good news:
Sleeping sickness can be cured with medicine if it is diagnosed early enough. Even in the later stages of the disease, it can be treated effectively. Most tsetse flies are not infected with the parasite that leads to sleeping sickness.

The bad news:
Sleeping sickness affects hundreds of thousands of people every year, and kills many of them. Without treatment you will almost certainly die. The medicines used in the treatment of the disease can themselves be dangerous. It's hard to tell the difference between a bite from a tsetse fly and a horsefly. There is no vaccine. Tsetse flies can cause other diseases in people too, and they are also responsible for a similar disease in cattle, which can wipe out entire herds.

FIELD AGENT REPORT

How to avoid deadly tsetse fly peril:

☠ Tsetse flies are active during the day, so make sure you apply insect repellent.

☠ Cover any exposed skin.

☠ Be alert for swollen lymph nodes—this could be a sign that you've been infected.

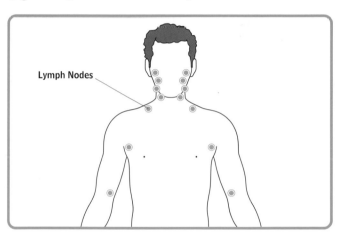

Lymph Nodes

Fact file:
Tsetse flies are yellow or brown bloodsucking flies, about half an inch long, found all over sub-Saharan Africa. There are more than 20 different species. The flies spread disease to animals and people by passing on microscopic parasites, known as trypanosomes. There are two forms of sleeping sickness, one spread in central and western Africa, the other in southern and eastern Africa, which is faster acting and considered the more dangerous of the two. The slower form of the disease, which can last for several years, is the one that's usually associated with the confused sleep patterns that give the disease its name.

Peril: Army Ants

Peril rating: 1/10

Location: Central and East Africa, and Asia

Best known for: Forming huge swarms that move in a relentless column to bring down, kill, and eat people in a matter of minutes

Your predicament:

You're in the Republic of Cameroon in Africa, staying in a hut on the edge of a village. Unfortunately, you have been struck down with a bad fever. You go to sleep, in the hope that when you wake up you will feel much better.

What's the worst that can happen?

Even more unfortunately for you, an enormous marching column of army ants is about to enter your hut and swarm over your weak, sleeping body . . .

1. You are so ill that you don't wake up as millions of ants swarm over you. Even if you did wake up, you wouldn't be able to move.
2. Some of the ants bite you; others swarm into your nostrils, ears, and mouth.
3. The ants choke you.
4. You die and are eaten by the ants.

The good news:

Contrary to what you might have heard, a swarm of army ants, however large, is not dangerous to humans unless there is some reason you can't move and there is no one around to help. In fact, people often welcome columns of army ants because they get rid of pests such as termites.

The bad news:

Army ants include soldier ants with large jaws that can inflict a painful bite. There can be tens of millions in a marching column. There are reports of weak, bedridden people being killed by army ants in Africa. There are other types of ants to worry about, including bullet ants, whose bite is so painful it's compared to the pain from a gunshot wound, and fire ants, which also have a painful bite and are aggressive.

FIELD AGENT REPORT

How to avoid deadly army ant peril:

☠ Apply insect repellent to exposed skin.

☠ Sleep underneath a mosquito net.

☠ If you are attacked by army ants, try not to panic, and walk quickly away from the main column, which travels at about 65 feet per hour.

Fact file:

Army ants is the name given to various different ant species that group together in large numbers to attack their prey. The ones found in Africa are known as army ants, driver ants, or siafu, and include many different species. Each colony can number many millions of ants, which leave the colony in an organized marching column when food supplies run low. The ants feed on insects and small animals. A different type of army ant is native to Central and South America.

PERILOUS WEATHER

You might think "bad weather"
means heavy snow or a
torrential downpour.
But truly perilous weather,
the kind that can uproot
trees, wash you away, or
freeze you to death, is only
a storm cloud away . . .

Peril: Lightning Strike
Peril rating: 4/10
Location: Worldwide
Best known for: Forking down from the heavens to incinerate unfortunate individuals

Your predicament:
There's a thunderstorm and you go down to the beach to watch it. You hear the roll of distant thunder and see lightning strikes, which appear to be getting closer all the time.

What's the worst that can happen?
You have greatly increased your chances of being struck by lightning by watching a thunderstorm close to a large expanse of water . . .

1. Lightning flashes dramatically down to the water some distance away.
2. You are the focus of the next strike.
3. A million volts course through your body, blasting you 30 feet into the air.
4. You die.

The good news:
Your chances of being struck by lightning are 1 in 3 million. Most people struck by lightning do not die—only between 10 and 20% of victims are killed. There is action you can take to avoid being struck by lightning.

The bad news:
Lightning can be very unpredictable and may strike up to 5 miles from the thunderstorm. Thunderstorms are common and can happen anywhere at any time. If you do survive a lightning strike, you are likely to have severe injuries.

FIELD AGENT REPORT

How to avoid deadly lightning peril:

☠ Don't be tempted to go outside and watch a thunderstorm.

☠ Don't stand near trees or any tall structures—these attract lightning (because they're an easier path to the earth than through the air).

☠ You're not completely safe in a car or a bus, but if you are inside one, don't get out.

☠ Metal is a good conductor of electricity: avoid it and also anything that makes you taller—e.g., golf clubs, fishing rods, or umbrellas.

☠ Water is a good conductor of electricity, so keep away from lakes, rivers, and the sea.

☠ You've a higher chance of surviving a lightning strike if you crouch down low, letting as little of your body as possible touch the ground.

☠ Count the seconds between seeing lightning and hearing thunder—if it's less than 30 seconds, the lightning is close enough to be a threat.

Fact file:

Lightning happens when negatively charged water droplets at the bottom of a thundercloud are attracted to the positively charged earth. The electrical charge will always follow the easiest route, so if there's anything above ground level that can conduct electricity, the lightning will use it—for example, a tall tree or building . . . or you, if you're close enough. On average there are 1,800 thunderstorms happening in the world at any given moment, with 100 lightning strikes per minute.

Peril: Tornado

Peril rating: 7/10

Location: Most parts of the world, but especially the United States

Best known for: Picking up people, vehicles, and buildings and dropping them from a great height

Your predicament:
You are in Oklahoma, the state most likely to experience powerful tornadoes. When you hear that one is on its way, your family decides to outrun it in a car, and do some storm-watching at the same time.

What's the worst that can happen?
Trying to outrun a tornado in a car is possibly the most stupid idea you have ever had—and it's to be your last . . .

1. You stop the car to watch the devastating tornado whirl around the countryside.
2. The tornado suddenly changes direction, heading directly for you.
3. You drive as fast as you can, but the tornado soon catches up with you.
4. The car is picked up, whirled high into the air, then flung down again several miles away.
5. You die.

The good news:
Only 2% of tornadoes are violent ones. If you are prepared and listen out for warnings, you should be fine—you only risk injury if you are out of doors, or in a car or trailer. Most tornadoes don't last very long.

The bad news:
Tornadoes produce the fastest winds on the planet and can't always be predicted. They can reach speeds of over 300 mph, and measure more than a mile across. Occasionally, tornadoes can continue a path of destruction for hundreds of miles. There are over a thousand tornadoes a year in the U.S.

FIELD AGENT REPORT

How to avoid deadly tornado peril:

☠ If you live in an area affected by tornadoes, have a disaster kit ready, including water, canned food, blankets, a first-aid kit, radio, and flashlight.

☠ Listen for tornado warnings on the radio or TV.

☠ If you're in a car or a mobile home, leave it (never try to outrun the tornado in a vehicle).

☠ Find shelter inside a building—preferably a basement, or the most central room on the lowest floor. Get underneath a sturdy table.

☠ Keep away from windows (and don't open them—it's a myth that the difference in pressure causes destruction).

Fact file:
A tornado is a violently spinning air column that descends from a thunderstorm to the ground. Tornadoes are smaller than hurricanes but more powerful. Inside a tornado is a calm "eye" of descending air. "Tornado Alley" (the band that runs down the center of the United States) experiences up to 700 per year. Waterspouts are formed when a tornado moves over water, sucking water upward. The largest one ever recorded was over half a mile high.

Peril: Blizzard

Peril rating: 5/10

Location: Cold and temperate regions worldwide

Best known for: Howling winds, driving snow, freezing cold

Your predicament:
You are hiking in the Alps. It is very cold and starts to snow.

What's the worst that can happen?
The relentless snow becomes thicker until it's impossible to tell the land from the sky. The harsh wind chills you to the bone. You become disoriented and decide to seek shelter . . .

1. You huddle beside a rocky outcrop.
2. After a while, you begin to shiver and feel numb in your hands and feet.
3. Your shivering becomes more violent. You try to walk around to warm up, but find it difficult to walk in a straight line. You become confused and have memory lapses.
4. You stop shivering. Your pulse is weak. You are extremely drowsy and fatigued.
5. You lose consciousness. Your heart and lungs fail while you sleep.
6. You die.

The good news:
It's possible to check for blizzard warnings and make advance preparations. If you have some survival training, your chances will be greatly improved. As long as you have a phone with you, you can call for help and tell rescuers where you are.

The bad news:
It's very easy to become disoriented in blizzard conditions. The weather can be unpredictable and catch you unawares. Cold can easily kill, even if you are wearing thermal clothing. You may also be in danger of frostbite, where blood vessels freeze and cause terrible damage, particularly to fingers and toes.

FIELD AGENT REPORT

How to avoid deadly blizzard peril:

☠ Listen up for blizzard warnings before you venture outside.

☠ Always tell someone what your plans are.

☠ If you are in a vehicle, stay inside. Turn on the engine for a few minutes every so often to provide heat.

☠ Always take a phone with you in mountainous regions (though it may not get a signal).

☠ Dress for the weather with plenty of warm layers, a hat, etc.

☠ Be prepared: take a change of clothing, nonperishable food, and a snow shovel.

☠ Don't eat snow—it will lower your body temperature. Melt it before drinking.

☠ Dig a snow cave if you can't find suitable shelter.

Fact file:

Blizzards are snowstorms with strong winds, low temperatures, heavy snow, and poor visibility. It can become very difficult to tell the earth from the sky (known as "whiteout") and deep snowdrifts are often formed.

Peril: Sandstorm

Peril rating: 3/10

Location: Dry regions worldwide

Best known for: Choking clouds of whirling sand and dust

Your predicament:

You're trekking across the Sahara Desert by camel on a hot, breezy day. The breeze becomes a strong, howling wind, heavy with dust and sand. The air starts to thicken. You look up and see a great yellow cloud swirling toward you.

What's the worst that can happen?

You are caught in the middle of a huge sandstorm . . .

1. Within minutes it becomes impossible to face the direction of the wind.
2. You can't see anything through the choking cloud.
3. You desperately look for shelter and soon become lost.
4. When the sandstorm clears, you have no idea where you are and your camels have disappeared.
5. For two days you search for an oasis or some kind of settlement, but find nothing.
6. You die of dehydration.

The good news:

Most sandstorms are small and last only a few minutes. If you're in a car, you will probably be able to outrun the storm—some sandstorms can travel at 65 mph but most are slower.

The bad news:

Sandstorms can be more than half a mile high and hundreds of miles wide, and can last many days. It's very easy to become lost in a sandstorm. The same conditions that cause sandstorms often cause thunderstorms too, so you may be in danger from lightning. The grains of sand can burn your skin if you're not well protected.

FIELD AGENT REPORT

How to avoid deadly sandstorm peril:

☠ Carry a mask to protect your mouth and nose, goggles for your eyes, and plenty of water.

☠ If you're in a group, make sure you all stay together—use a rope if necessary.

☠ Your camel is far better adapted to conditions in a sandstorm than you are. Use your four-legged friend as shelter.

☠ Don't take shelter behind a sand dune— whole dunes can be picked up by the storm. Find a rock instead.

☠ Because the sand and dust particles in a sandstorm are denser lower down, move to higher ground. However, if the storm is accompanied by thunder and lightning, stay lower down so as not to expose yourself to a lightning strike.

Fact file:

Sandstorms happen when strong winds blow over loose sand or earth. In deserts, there are more sandstorms at particular times of year, when hot air causes powerful winds close to the ground. The storms can also be caused by deforestation and poor farming methods. Sandstorms occur in North Africa, the Middle East, the southwestern United States, and China.

Peril: Flash Flood

Peril rating: 7/10

Location: Worldwide

Best known for: Crashing through valleys without warning and sweeping away everything in its path

Your predicament:
You are camping in a French valley in the foothills of the Pyrenees. There's a sudden violent thunderstorm.

What's the worst that can happen?
You notice that a mountain stream has become a torrent and decide to head out of the valley and back to the nearest town . . .

1. Just as you set off, you hear a roaring sound: a deluge rushes down the valley.
2. There is nowhere for you to run—you are caught in the path of the approaching flash flood.
3. Tangled up in the rushing wall of water are branches and other debris.
4. They slam into you, killing you instantly.

The good news:
Flash floods are not common—usually you would have some warning of a possible flood.

The bad news:
Floods cause more damage than any other natural phenomenon. By their nature, flash floods take people by surprise. If you do not drown, you may be killed by floating debris.

FIELD AGENT REPORT

How to avoid deadly flash flood peril:

☠ If heavy rain is forecast, avoid deep valleys.

☠ If you can see a flood approaching, try to head for higher ground.

☠ If it catches up with you, find something that floats to hang on to. If possible, cling to a strong tree by the bank.

☠ If your phone is working, use it to call for help.

☠ Signal for rescue with a mirror.

Fact file:

Flash floods happen within a few hours (most other floods develop over many hours or days). They are usually caused by sudden storms, but might also come about because of a burst dam.

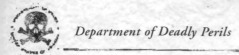

Peril: Freak Wave

Peril rating: 3/10

Location: Worldwide

Best known for: Appearing out of nowhere to destroy large ships

Your predicament:
You are on a cruise ship off the east coast of South Africa close to the notorious Agulhas Current. The sea is quite rough, but suddenly a single enormous wave rises in front of the ship, seemingly out of nowhere.

What's the worst that can happen?
You look on in terror as the wave draws nearer, and see that there is a deep trough in front of it. The wave looks almost vertical and more than 65 feet high . . .

1. The enormous wall of water bears down on the ship.
2. Because the wave is so steep, the ship can't climb it. The wave breaks over the ship.
3. The huge pressure of the water destroys navigation and other equipment and capsizes the ship.
4. You drown.

The good news:
Ships have weathered freak waves and survived. Freak waves are more likely in certain areas and conditions, so warnings can be given or shipping rerouted (for example, off the South African coast when winds are blowing contrary to the Agulhas Current, or off the coast of Norway in stormy weather). Reports of freak waves are rare.

The bad news:
No ship is designed to withstand waves of 65 to 95 feet. Recent satellite data showed ten waves 80 feet or higher in a three-week period worldwide. The waves can appear without warning, and sometimes come in threes. Though reports of freak waves are not common, this may be because few survive to make reports.

FIELD AGENT REPORT

How to avoid deadly wave peril:

☠ Get inside and move to the part of the ship that's farthest away from the wave.

☠ If you're not already wearing one, put on a life jacket.

☠ Hang on to something solid, or strap yourself to it if possible.

☠ Stay away from windows.

Fact file:

Freak waves are not just large waves in stormy seas: they are huge, solitary waves, much larger than the other waves, that appear without warning out at sea. No one knows for certain what causes them. There are various theories: storm waves running into strong currents flowing in the opposite direction (though not all freak waves occur in strong currents); or several waves interracting with one another; or shallow water focusing waves into one spot, causing one very large wave.

Peril: Giant Hail

Peril rating: 3/10

Location: Worldwide in cold and temperate regions

Best known for: Freezing and sometimes deadly aerial bombardment

Your predicament:

You're out walking on the Yorkshire moors in the U.K. in winter. The wind picks up, thunder rumbles, and it starts to rain, which soon turns to icy sleet.

What's the worst that can happen?

You trudge miserably toward the nearest shelter half a mile or so away. Suddenly you feel a thump as you are hit on the back by a large hailstone. You start to run . . .

1. With no shelter, you are entirely exposed to the lumps of ice as they rain down.
2. You notice they are starting to increase in size.
3. One especially big hailstone, the size of an orange, hits you on the head.
4. You die instantly.

The good news:

Death by giant hail is very rare. The bigger the hailstone, the fewer of them will fall. People have been struck by giant hail and not suffered any lasting injury.

The bad news:

Being hit on the head by a falling object weighing 2 pounds or more, at a speed approaching 60 mph, is more than enough to kill you. People can and do get killed by giant hail—your chances of survival depend on whether or not you have access to shelter.

FIELD AGENT REPORT

How to avoid deadly giant hail peril:

☠ Stay indoors during severe storms and keep away from windows, which could be shattered by a large hailstone.

☠ If you are caught outside, locate shelter as quickly as possible—preferably not under a tree, as they also attract lightning.

☠ Don't put up an umbrella, for similar reasons.

☠ In a car, stop and huddle to the middle, away from windows. Put a coat or other covering over your head to protect you in case a window breaks.

Fact file:

Hailstones are solid balls of ice that form inside thunderclouds. They start as small specks of dirt that build up layers of ice around them. When the hailstone is too heavy to be supported by the updraft of the thunderstorm, it falls. The thunderstorms that produce hailstones have to have very strong updrafts. Often, hailstones fall and are then pushed upward again in another strong updraft, increasing in size each time they do so. Because ice is heavy, hailstones can cause a lot of damage. The biggest hailstone ever recorded was 7 inches in diameter.

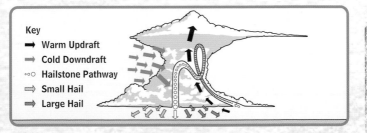

Key
→ Warm Updraft
⇒ Cold Downdraft
°°○ Hailstone Pathway
⇨ Small Hail
⇨ Large Hail

Peril: Hurricane
Peril rating: 8/10
Location: Worldwide
Best known for: Being the most powerful storms on the planet

Your predicament:
You are on vacation in Mexico during hurricane season. A hurricane warning is given, but you decide not to worry about it, and join other partiers in a "hurricane party" in a beachfront apartment instead.

What's the worst that can happen?
As you and your friends watch the storm through the window, it becomes increasingly clear that this hurricane isn't anything to celebrate . . .

1. You watch fearfully as trees are toppled, cars are overturned, and the torrential rain causes flooding.
2. Powerful winds fling a large branch at the window of your apartment.
3. You are hit by flying debris and glass.
4. You die.

The good news:
Scientists can track hurricanes and work out roughly where they are headed, so usually you would have plenty of warning. There is action you can take to keep safe during a hurricane.

The bad news:
Hurricanes are immensely powerful and highly dangerous. As Earth's climate warms, they are becoming more common. The path of a hurricane can't be predicted accurately. Power lines may be brought down in a hurricane, which can be lethal, especially when the ground is wet.

FIELD AGENT REPORT

How to avoid deadly hurricane peril:

☠ If there's a hurricane warning and you are told to evacuate, do so as quickly as possible. Pack plenty of water, a first-aid kit, blankets, clothes, etc., and head inland.

☠ If you are indoors during a hurricane, stay there. Go to the middle of the building, away from windows.

☠ If there's time, board windows or close shutters.

Fact file:

Hurricanes form out at sea, when warm air rises upward, sucking in more air, which spins and builds into a spiral of thunderclouds. Hurricanes occur in tropical areas near the equator, usually between June and November. A powerful hurricane might be 300 miles across, with wind speeds of up to 190 mph and torrential rain. Winds rotate around a calm area in the middle—the "eye" of the storm. In the Atlantic and Caribbean they are called hurricanes, in the Pacific they are called typhoons, and in the Indian Ocean they're known as cyclones.

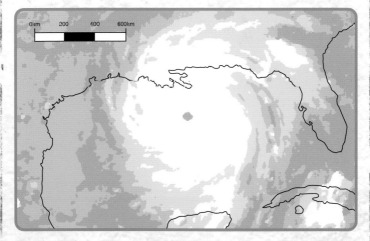

EVERYDAY PERILS

If you're going to have an accident,
it's most likely going to be at home.
Taking a bath, getting dressed,
and even sleeping are in fact
all fraught with DANGER.

Peril: Getting Dressed

Peril rating: 1/10

Location: Worldwide

Best known for: Not really being remotely dangerous

Your predicament:

You had to get up extra early and are still half-asleep. There's no time for a shower. You manage to find some clothes and put one foot in the leg of a pair of jeans.

What's the worst that can happen?

It is not your lucky day . . .

1. As you put the other foot in, you lose your balance and go hopping across the room.
2. You topple over and hit your head on the corner of a bedside table.
3. You die instantly.

The good news:

Even if you do fall over or otherwise injure yourself getting dressed, you are extremely unlikely to die as a result. Clothing generally has few sharp elements that are likely to cause you serious harm. Injuries while getting dressed usually happen to small children, for obvious reasons.

The bad news:

Accidents while getting dressed are very common. It's not just falling over while putting on clothing or footwear that can be hazardous (note: rubber boots are a common cause of injury). You can hurt yourself zipping up your clothes, with flesh becoming painfully stuck. There are more accidents involving pants than there are accidents involving chain saws.

FIELD AGENT REPORT

How to avoid deadly clothing peril:

☠ Make sure you get dressed with the light on to minimize risk of balance loss.

☠ Tidy up—a pair of pants left on an uncarpeted, shiny floor is an accident waiting to happen.

☠ Change clothes less frequently. Changing every six months should seriously reduce your risk of clothing-related injury. But it might also reduce your popularity!

Fact file:

According to the U.S. Centers for Disease Control and Prevention, there are hundreds of thousands of unintentional accidents in which victims seek hospital care every year. In Great Britain, in the last year of recorded figures, more than 5,000 accidents involved pants and more than 11,000 were due to socks or tights. And in recent years in the U.K., clothing and footwear injuries have accounted for about eight times the number of accidents involving DIY tools and machinery.

Peril: Electricity
Peril rating: 8/10
Location: Worldwide
Best known for: Being an invisible but extremely dangerous hazard in the home

Your predicament:
You are on vacation and decide to go back to the hotel for a long bath before going out. Your hair dryer is on the shelf above the tub.

What's the worst that can happen?
You know that electricity and water don't mix, but you've heard that anything electrical would have to be switched on before falling into the bath in order for it to be dangerous. Unfortunately, this is about to be put to the test . . .

1. The hair dryer slips off the steam-coated shelf and into the bath.
2. The hair dryer is plugged into the power socket. Although it is not switched on, faulty wiring causes the appliance to electrify the bath water . . .
3. You die.

The good news:
Modern electrical equipment is very safe, as are modern power sockets, plugs, etc. There would need to be something wrong with an appliance for it to cause an electric shock in this way. Most modern homes have an electrical circuit breaker fitted in the bathroom and kitchen, which would prevent someone being electrocuted.

The bad news:
Hundreds of deaths occur every year due to accidents with electricity. Electrical problems account for thousands of fires every year, with many more lives lost. Old appliances can easily be dangerous. If your house hasn't been rewired recently, it could be hiding various electrical perils.

FIELD AGENT REPORT

How to avoid deadly electrical peril:

☠ Don't use portable electrical appliances in the bathroom.

☠ Don't use any electrical appliance that has a damaged cord.

☠ Make sure there are electrical circuit breakers fitted in the house, especially in the bathroom and kitchen.

☠ The wiring in a house should be checked by a qualified electrician once every five years.

☠ Don't overload electrical sockets.

☠ Never clean an electrical appliance while it's plugged in.

☠ Never touch someone who has been electrocuted without turning off the power source or moving them away from it with something that doesn't conduct electricity, e.g., a plastic or wooden broom handle.

☠ Don't run electrical leads underneath carpets—they can overheat and cause fires.

Fact file:

Electricity is created when electrons move from atom to atom. The electricity we use is produced in power plants using energy from water, wind, coal, etc. It powers many of the everyday things we do, yet it's potentially lethal. Metal is a very good conductor of electricity, which is why electrical wires are made of metal. Water is another good electrical conductor—and since our bodies are made up mostly of water, they are good conductors too.

Peril: **Poisonous Garden Plant**

Peril rating: 4/10

Location: Temperate and tropical regions worldwide

Best known for: Poisoning unwary gardeners

Your predicament:

You gather some lettuce from the vegetable patch to make a salad. You add some flowers—you've heard that nasturtiums have a peppery taste and they look nice. The pink flowers of an oleander bush look so pretty you decide to add those too, along with some leaves.

What's the worst that can happen?

As it turns out, you've added one of the most poisonous plants on the planet to your salad . . .

1. Unaware of the dreadful fate that awaits you, you happily consume several oleander flowers.
2. Soon after you've finished, you feel sick.
3. You have a terrible stomachache and start to vomit.
4. Your heart beats very fast, then becomes erratic.
5. You lose consciousness.
6. You die.

The good news:

As long as you're not silly enough to eat a plant you don't know anything about, you won't be in deadly peril in the first place. You stand a good chance of surviving poisoning by oleander as long as you seek medical attention quickly, and as long as you are not a small child. Cases of oleander poisoning are very rare.

The bad news:

Oleander is one of the most poisonous plants in the world. The whole plant is poisonous, even dried leaves. A handful of leaves is enough to kill an adult human, and there are even reports of people being killed by the poison because they used oleander twigs to spit-roast meat. There are plenty of other common garden plants that can kill you (see opposite page).

FIELD AGENT REPORT

How to avoid deadly garden plant peril:

☠ Don't eat the leaves, fruit, flowers, or any part of a plant if you're not sure it's safe.

☠ Wear gloves while gardening.

☠ If you think you have eaten a poisonous plant, get to a doctor immediately, taking part of the plant with you for identification.

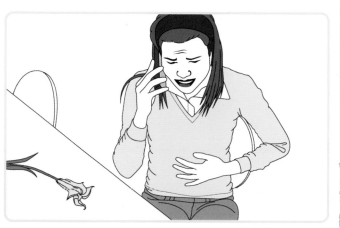

Fact file:

Oleander is an evergreen shrub grown all over the world—in warmer parts of the world it's often planted in public places because it's easy to grow. It contains a range of different toxins. There are many different garden plants that can be very dangerous if eaten, even in small quantities, including foxgloves, castor oil plants, and aconites. Deadly nightshade is an ordinary-looking plant, often found in woodland and sometimes in gardens, that has tasty-looking black berries: it is also extremely poisonous (10 to 20 berries is enough to kill an adult).

Peril: Sleepwalking

Peril rating: 2/10

Location: Worldwide

Best known for: Causing sleeping people to crash zombie-like through plate-glass windows with outstretched arms

Your predicament:
After a long-haul flight, you go to bed absolutely exhausted, feeling tense because you have an important exam coming up.

What's the worst that can happen?
You soon fall into a deep sleep . . .

1. Only 30 minutes or so after you've fallen asleep, you get up again—without waking.
2. You shamble from the bedroom and downstairs, narrowly avoiding a headlong fall.
3. You open the front door and stagger into the road, where you are run over by a passing car.
4. You die.

The good news:
Sleepwalking is not usually dangerous, let alone fatal. Most sleepwalkers don't sleepwalk very often. If you do have a history of sleepwalking, you can take action to make sure you don't injure yourself.

The bad news:
Injuries to sleepwalkers are common because sleepwalkers don't see their surroundings in a normal way: they may think they are somewhere quite different and trip over furniture, walk into doors, etc. People will sometimes perform complicated and potentially dangerous tasks while sleepwalking, such as moving heavy furniture, or even climbing to the top of a crane (in one case). You don't have to have a history of sleepwalking—it can happen to someone who has never sleepwalked before.

FIELD AGENT REPORT

How to avoid deadly sleepwalking peril:

☠ If you're a sleepwalker, make sure you don't have easy access to anything potentially dangerous (knives, car keys, etc.).

☠ Lock windows and doors, and block access to stairs.

☠ Sleep on the ground floor if possible.

☠ Make sure windows are covered with thick curtains.

☠ Learn some relaxation exercises and make sure you get plenty of sleep.

☠ If sleepwalking is putting you at risk of injury, see a doctor— it might be possible to prevent your sleepwalking with medication.

Fact file:
Sleepwalking is more common in children. It's also more common among people who have high stress levels. Sleepwalking usually happens within the first few hours of going to bed and takes place during deep sleep—not while dreaming. People usually have their eyes wide open when they sleepwalk and may be muttering unintelligibly. They won't be able to respond normally to others, and afterward won't remember what happened while they were sleepwalking.

Peril: Botulism

Peril rating: 4/10

Location: Worldwide

Best known for: Being caused by the deadliest naturally occurring nerve toxin known to science

Your predicament:
In search of a snack one evening you resort to sampling Auntie Mildred's home-canned green beans.

What's the worst that can happen?
Auntie Mildred's beans were contaminated with deadly bacteria and you are now infected with botulism. Around lunchtime the following day . . .

1. You start to feel tired and weak.
2. You experience the symptoms of muscle paralysis, such as blurred vision, drooping eyelids, and slurred speech.
3. You assume you must have a bug and go to bed to sleep it off. Gradually, muscles all over your body become paralyzed.
4. The muscles that control breathing are affected.
5. You die.

The good news:
Botulism is quite rare, and in most cases victims survive—deaths from botulism account for only about 8% of cases. If diagnosed early, botulism can be treated with an antitoxin. The toxin produced by the botulinum bacterium is destroyed at high temperatures, so steps can be taken to avoid it in the preparation of food.

The bad news:
The botulin toxin is one of the strongest and most deadly poisons in the world. Canned food is especially in danger of becoming contaminated unless strict guidelines are followed in its preparation, and there have been cases of botulism from commercially prepared canned foods and preserves. Botulism can be difficult to diagnose because the symptoms are shared with other conditions. It takes a long time to recover from botulism—severe cases may need several months of medical care. Patients may find that they are short of breath and easily tired for years after the illness. Outbreaks of food-borne botulism happen most years.

FIELD AGENT REPORT

How to avoid deadly botulism peril:

☠ If you are canning food at home, make sure the food is heated for at least ten minutes at a temperature higher than 185° F.

☠ Don't eat any canned food if the can looks swollen.

☠ If you have symptoms of muscle paralysis, get medical treatment right away. Patients with botulism may need a ventilator.

Fact file:

The bacteria that cause botulism are commonly found in soil. The three most common ways of getting the illness are: by eating food infected with the toxin; by eating the bacteria, which then grows in the intestine and produces the toxin (this can happen to children under a year old—older children and adults have developed a defense against the bacteria); or by a wound becoming infected with the toxin. The bacteria can be present in honey, so children under a year old shouldn't eat it. The toxin can be diluted and used to paralyze muscles in medical and cosmetic treatments: this is known as Botox.

ADVENTUROUS PERILS

If getting dressed is an
accident waiting to happen,
what perils lie in wait for the
adventurous? From scuba diving to
parachuting, adventurous activities
bring with them all sorts of
terrible calamities that
could befall you . . .

Peril: The Bends

Peril rating: 5/10

Location: Worldwide

Best known for: Causing agonizing death to scuba divers

Your predicament:

You're diving in the Red Sea at a depth of about 100 feet when you spot a passing lemon shark. It looks dangerous. You swim away from the shark and upward, panic causing you to pay little regard to the dive table charts you have memorized.

What's the worst that can happen?

You have surfaced too quickly. You go to bed, assuming you have a migraine, but an hour or two later . . .

1. You experience severe pain in your joints. This is known as "the bends" and is caused by nitrogen being released into joints and muscles.
2. Your skin itches and you develop a rash.
3. Your neck and body begin to hurt too.
4. You also experience "the chokes"—coughing and chest pain—and "the staggers"—dizziness and deafness.
5. Unable to get to medical help or to a recompression chamber on your own, you die.

The good news:

The depths for most recreational dives are safe. There are various treatments available that will cure the bends. If you are fairly young and fit, the chances of recovery are good even if there is a delay in getting to a recompression chamber.

The bad news:

If there is no means of getting to a recompression chamber, decompression sickness (which causes symptoms such as the bends, the chokes, etc.) may well be fatal. It is extremely painful. If you don't die, you may end up with irreversible damage to your joints. There are other dangers in scuba diving, running out of air, nitrogen narcosis, and oxygen toxicity among them.

FIELD AGENT REPORT

How to avoid deadly diving peril:

☠ Make sure you follow dive tables, which show you how long it is safe to stay at particular depths.

☠ To surface safely from a deep dive, come up slowly and in stages.

☠ If you do rise too quickly, you should be given oxygen within four hours of the dive.

☠ Get to a hospital or recompression chamber as soon as possible.

☠ Don't fly directly after diving. Depending on the depth and length of your dive, you may have to wait between 12 and 48 hours before flying.

☠ Drink plenty of water—this will make your blood better able to cope with nitrogen bubbles.

☠ If you are diving deeply, try a different mixture of gases that contains less nitrogen.

Fact file:

The bends is one of the symptoms of decompression sickness, which is caused by high-pressure gas inside the body. If the diver swims to the surface without making stops to "decompress," nitrogen gas is released into the diver's body too quickly, like bubbles in a soda bottle rising suddenly to the surface.

Peril: Altitude Sickness

Peril rating: 4/10

Location: Mountainous regions worldwide

Best known for: Striking down fit, healthy climbers

Your predicament:
You're trekking in Tibet, in the foothills of the mighty Himalayas.

What's the worst that can happen?
Against advice, you've climbed more quickly than recommended. One night, six hours or so after the end of your day's climb, you start to feel ill . . .

1. You have a terrible headache that won't go away when you take painkillers.
2. You feel weak and tired and start to vomit.
3. You are experiencing the symptoms of acute altitude sickness. This often goes away after a day or so, but in your case, unfortunately, it develops into High Altitude Cerebral Edema (HACE).
4. You start to lose your memory. You have hallucinations.
5. You fall into a coma.
6. You die.

The good news:
There is not much likelihood of acute altitude sickness developing into a more serious, life-threatening condition. If you experience altitude sickness, it can be treated easily by descending. Most people can ascend to around 8,200 feet without symptoms. Even if you do develop a life-threatening condition such as HACE, it can be treated as long as you get medical attention quickly.

The bad news:
Some people are more susceptible to altitude sickness than others, regardless of how fit they are. HACE and HAPE (High Altitude Pulmonary Edema) are extremely dangerous and often fatal. There are extra hazards associated with high altitude: the air is very dry, which can make you cough so violently that your ribs fracture; you are also in danger of dehydration because of greater loss of water vapor from the lungs at high altitudes.

FIELD AGENT REPORT

How to avoid deadly altitude sickness peril:

☠ Ascend slowly to give your body time to adjust.

☠ If you are over 9,000 feet up, don't ascend more than 950 feet in one day.

☠ If you ascend 3,000 feet in three consecutive days, spend one day resting.

☠ Drink lots of fluid—1 gallon a day is recommended.

☠ To avoid a violent cough at high altitudes, breathe through clothing or a mask.

☠ Avoid flying or driving to high altitudes, and don't move up any higher for the first 24 hours.

☠ If you do feel ill, descend as soon as possible.

☠ For more serious conditions such as HACE, medication and hospitalization will be necessary.

Fact file:

Acute altitude sickness occurs above about 8,200 feet, and serious symptoms don't usually occur until about 11,500 to 13,000 feet. The causes are not fully understood, but most of the symptoms are the result of low carbon dioxide levels, which change the PH level of the blood. High altitude and lower air pressure can also lead to a build-up of fluid in the lungs and the brain.

Peril: Skydiving
Peril rating: 2/10
Location: Worldwide
Best known for: Parachutes that fail to open

Your predicament:
It's your first ever free-fall parachute jump—this means you will fall several thousand feet before you open your parachute. You summon all your courage and leap from the plane, mentally revisiting all the safety information you have learned.

What's the worst that can happen?
Once clear of the plane, you count to ten and pull the cord on your parachute. To your utter horror, the chute fails to open . . .

1. You can't think of anything except the fact that you are plummeting toward the ground very quickly indeed.
2. Fear makes you black out.
3. You hit the ground at a speed of hundreds of yards per second.
4. You die.

The good news:
All parachute jumps are made with a reserve chute in addition to the main one; you will have been taught how to open it. Some parachutes have a safety system that makes them open automatically when close to the ground and falling fast. It's possible for another, experienced skydiver to rescue someone whose parachute hasn't opened. Accidents are rare and are not usually caused by equipment malfunction, but because of a deliberate risk taken by the skydiver. The likelihood of being killed skydiving is very small.

The bad news:
Even though the risk is small, if your chutes do fail to open for any reason you are extremely unlikely to survive a fall of several thousand yards. Changing wind conditions can be dangerous—there may be a sudden downdraft. The flight before the jump, and even the airfield itself, also carry their own risks.

FIELD AGENT REPORT

How to avoid deadly skydiving peril:

☠ If you are young and healthy, you stand a better chance of skydiving without injury.

☠ Listen to your instructors and follow their safety advice meticulously.

☠ Always check your equipment thoroughly before a jump.

☠ Don't jump if you are feeling unwell.

☠ If anything does go wrong, don't panic! You will have been trained in how to deal with an emergency.

Fact file:

A skydiver's reserve parachute is regularly checked by someone appropriately qualified, whether or not it has been used. In the basic free-fall position, skydivers plummet toward the earth at a rate of 115 mph. Injury rates are low, even for novices—about one injury in 125 jumps, and two or three deaths per 100,000 jumps.

Peril: Shipwreck

Peril rating: 2/10

Location: Seas worldwide

Best known for: Marooning lone victims on remote desert islands

Your predicament:
You are on board a ship in the midst of a raging gale. The ship becomes battered and broken and unable to cope with the high seas. The captain gives the order to abandon ship.

What's the worst that can happen?
You make it to a life raft with other passengers. There's time to grab some water and food, but the raft is an old, ill-equipped one . . .

1. The storm carries you far away from the ship—and from rescuers.
2. You are completely disoriented. You allow the raft to drift, hoping to find land.
3. Despite signaling with mirrors, you see no other craft.
4. Days pass and no land is sighted. Your meager supplies begin to dwindle.
5. There is limited shade for all the passengers.
6. Eventually, the water runs out.
7. After weeks of drifting, you die of dehydration.

The good news:
Modern life rafts have high sides, an insulated bottom, buckets for bailing, signaling and fishing equipment, ladders, repair kits, desalinators, anchors, and paddles. People can survive for months adrift on rafts at sea, using primitive fishing rods to catch fish, and collecting rainwater for drinking. People have also survived for years on desert islands before being rescued. Unless you are a regular sailor, your chances of being shipwrecked are remote.

The bad news:
You can easily die of exposure in a life raft—either because of excessive heat or the cold and wet. A small boat in the open sea offers little protection from rough weather. Sharks have been known to prey on small drifting rafts. In the open ocean, a life raft can be extremely difficult to spot.

FIELD AGENT REPORT

How to avoid deadly shipwreck peril:

☠ Stay in the shade during the day.

☠ Collect rainwater and dew by hanging a tarpaulin.

☠ Watch out for signs of land: they include fluffy clouds with flat bottoms, seals, and flocks of birds (try to follow their evening direction).

☠ Don't drink seawater.

If you make it to a desert island:

☠ Look for water—always filter it and boil it.

☠ Look for a rocky overhang or fallen tree and use branches and leaves to turn it into a shelter. Line it with dry vegetation for warmth.

☠ Gather kindling and use a lens, or two sticks rubbed together, to make fire.

☠ Don't eat any plants you aren't sure are edible. Make a spear or fishing rod from sticks, string, or reed and whatever metal objects you have on hand.

☠ Create an SOS sign out of rocks.

Fact file:

Ships have been wrecked due to bad weather, navigation error, or collision since people first went to sea, and there's evidence of the wreckage all over the world. The most famous shipwreck is of the passenger liner RMS *Titanic*, which sank on its first ever voyage in 1912 when it hit an iceberg.

Peril: Cave-in

Peril rating: 6/10

Location: Worldwide

Best known for: Entombing cavers within mountains of rubble

Your predicament:

You are caving with two others in the Peak District of northern England. You hear the sound of some falling gravel up ahead of you, followed by some large rocks clattering down the side of the cave toward you.

What's the worst that can happen?

You duck for cover, but the rockfall is a serious one . . .

1. You and your two companions have all been injured by the rocks as they fell and are unable to start clearing a route through the debris.
2. You told someone aboveground where you were going, but failed to leave precise instructions about when you would be back, or what they should do if you don't contact them.
3. It's cold and damp. You begin to shiver and are soon showing signs of hypothermia.
4. You die.

The good news:

Rockfalls inside caves are rare. If you are caught and injured in a rockfall, the chances are that one of your companions will be able to get out and find help.

The bad news:

Rockfalls can easily trap you in a cave or kill you outright. There are plenty of other caving hazards to worry about, such as flooding, or the cold and damp (which puts you at risk of hypothermia). You might also get lost, fall down a deep drop, or get stuck in a narrow passage.

FIELD AGENT REPORT

How to avoid deadly cave peril:

☠ Never go caving alone—three people is the absolute minimum (so that if someone is injured, one person can stay with him or her while the third person goes for help). The group must stay together.

☠ Tell someone where you are going to be caving and when you expect to be back. If all else fails and you and your fellow cavers are in trouble and unable to get out of the cave, this is your only hope of rescue.

☠ Have a backup flashlight, plus another light source, and bring spare batteries and bulbs.

☠ Make sure you're wearing the right clothing, including a hard hat.

☠ If you do get into trouble, don't panic—panicking inside a confined space is definitely not going to help.

Fact file:

The most common type of caves are solution caves, which have been hollowed out by water over a very long time—they very rarely collapse, though rockfalls are possible. Caving and potholing (potholes are vertical caves) are popular sports, despite the dangers—mainly hypothermia, flooding, and falling down steep drops. Rescuing cavers who are trapped or injured is difficult and time-consuming, and rescuers need specialist training.

DON'T PANIC!

By this time, you'll probably have reached the conclusion that deadly peril isn't really very likely to come your way at all. That is, unless you insist on surfing alone at dusk in an area where large sharks are known to feed, chasing a tornado, or canoeing past an angry hippopotamus.

It's comforting to realize that we can cross many perils off our list of things to worry about: piranha fish (which won't reduce you to a skeleton within seconds, as previously thought), quicksand (far from being the treacherous pit of doom you'd imagined), and falling coconuts (widely held to claim more victims than sharks).

Admittedly, you've probably read about perils that previously hadn't worried you at all: plummeting tortoises, solar flares, and garden plants, perhaps. But you should feel safe in the knowledge that tortoises usually stay on the ground, Earth has a useful magnetic field, and most plants we grow are completely harmless.

While the world can be full of perils, at least now you know what they are—and how to avoid them.

WITHDRAWN

About the author:

Tracey Turner writes books for children
and adults about lots of different subjects,
including famous writers, rude words,
mysterious sliding rocks, and, of course,
deadly perils. When she's not escaping
perilous situations, she lives in Bath,
England, with Tom and their son, Toby.

About the illustrator:

Ben Hasler studied art and design before
specializing in illustration. He joined the WhiteRoom at
the award-winning HHCL and Partners Agency, where
he established WRIP (WhiteRoom Illustrators Portfolio).
He is now a freelancer and splits his time between
Brighton, England, and Brazil.